# JOURNEY TO WEALTH INFINITY

Empowering Kids in Money Management
and Wealth-Building Habits

TALANKI NAVEEN KUMAR GUPTHA

ISBN
Paperback  979-8-89610-736-1
Hardcase  979-8-89699-333-9

# Contents

# Contents

. . . . . . . . . . . . . . . . . . . . . . . . . . . . . . . . . . . . . . . . . .

This book is dedicated to my family: my loving wife,
Asha, and my amazing daughters, Vritika, Saavni,
and Manasvi.


"Wealth isn't a destination; it's a journey of learning,
growing, and creating a legacy that endures."


— Talanki Naveen Kumar Guptha, CMA

. . . . . . . . . . . . . . . . . . . . . . . . . . . . . . . . . . . . . . . . . .

# Foreword

As we navigate an era of rapid financial change and an increasingly complex world, the importance of financial literacy cannot be overstated. This book, ***Journey to Wealth Infinity: Empowering Kids in Money Management and Wealth-Building Habits,*** serves as a powerful guide in that journey, not only for young minds but for anyone looking to build a foundation in financial education.

Reflecting on my own path, I recognise how small, consistent actions can transform one's financial future. From the habit of saving pocket money to making thoughtful investments, these lessons go beyond money – they instil discipline, resilience, and the power of long-term thinking. In the world of finance, time is often the greatest asset. Teaching children to start early grants them a valuable advantage, allowing them to harness the power of compounding and make decisions that grow their wealth sustainably.

In this book, readers are introduced to foundational concepts of saving, budgeting, and investing through relatable stories and practical steps. By demystifying finance, this book empowers young readers and their mentors to embark on a journey toward financial independence. I believe that as we raise a financially aware generation, we lay the groundwork for a more prosperous society.

May this book inspire the habit of lifelong learning and financial empowerment in all who read it.

Warm regards,

**Vivek Mashrani, CFA**

# Preface

Looking back now, I see how a simple habit—setting aside a few coins each week—planted the seeds for a lifelong journey towards financial independence. At the time, I didn't understand the power of those small actions, but they were quietly teaching me lessons about consistency, discipline, and growth. Years later, these principles guided me from a career in finance to becoming a full-time trader and investor, shaping not only my life but also my vision for empowering others.

*Journey to Wealth Infinity* was born out of a desire to share these foundational lessons with the next generation and those guiding it. This book introduces a concept I call the "Wealth Infinity Cycle" – a cycle of growth and reinvestment that starts with the basics of saving and expands into disciplined investing, compounding, and financial independence. I believe that every child deserves the opportunity to learn these principles early, not necessarily to become rich, but to become free.

This book is written for parents and teachers who understand that financial literacy is a skill as important as any academic subject. My goal is to provide a resource that makes teaching and learning about money accessible, practical, and enjoyable. In a world where financial decisions come earlier than ever, equipping children with the right knowledge, habits, and mindset can give them a lifetime advantage.

Throughout the pages that follow, you'll find stories, examples, and simple steps to start your own journey toward financial freedom. With each chapter, I encourage readers to make the lessons their own, whether through simple savings goals or the first steps into low-risk investing. Every small step is a vital part of the journey – a journey that, if begun early, can grow into a legacy.

Thank you for joining me on this path. Together, let's nurture the next generation of financially aware, resilient, and empowered individuals. This is their journey, their wealth, and their future. Let's make it infinite.

Talanki Naveen Kumar Guptha, CMA (The Institute of Cost Accountants of India)

# Acknowledgements

I would like to express my profound gratitude to the remarkable individuals who have contributed to the creation of this book.

First and foremost, I am deeply indebted to **Dr. Manjunath**, Mind Performance Coach, whose inspiration and expertise were instrumental in encouraging me to write this book focusing on the core area. His insights into mental performance and coaching have significantly shaped the direction of this work.

I extend my heartfelt thanks to **Mr. Vivek Mashrani**, CFA, for sharing his profound knowledge of the financial markets and for encouraging resilience in my stock market journey. His insights have been invaluable, and I am honoured to have his support through the foreword in this book.

Special appreciation goes to **Mr. Naresh Gaddapati**, an alumnus of the prestigious Indian Institute of Technology (IIT) Roorkee M.Tech Chemical Engineering. His meticulous attention to detail and analytical mindset have been invaluable in reviewing this work.

I extend my deepest appreciation to **Mr. P.S.R. Mitraji**, a distinguished educator who taught accounting and allied subjects at Hindu College, Machilipatnam, and Rishi Valley School (K.F.I.), Madanapalle. His profound understanding of financial planning, shaped by decades of experience and personal observation, has been an invaluable asset in reviewing this book. His insightful feedback and thoughtful suggestions have significantly enhanced the manuscript, ensuring it is both practical and impactful for readers.

A particularly heartfelt acknowledgment goes to my daughter, **Talanki Vritika Guptha,** whose fresh perspective and honest feedback have made this book more relatable and engaging for a wide audience. Her enthusiasm and curiosity have been a constant source of inspiration.

I also want to acknowledge the role of Artificial Intelligence tools in enhancing the writing process. These modern technologies provided valuable assistance in organising and refining the content while maintaining the authenticity of the ideas presented.

# Introduction

# Why Financial Literacy for Kids Matters

In today's fast-paced world, teaching children about money early on is more important than ever. While most kids learn basic math, science, and language skills in school, they rarely get a formal education on financial literacy – something that will impact their entire lives. The habits, skills, and mindset that children develop around money will shape their future success, independence, and security.

This book, *Journey to Wealth Infinity: Empowering Kids in Money Management and Wealth-Building Habits*, is designed to help parents and teachers instil in children not only the practical skills they need to start saving and investing but also the broader mindset needed to develop long-term wealth. It's not just about teaching kids how to save money or invest in stocks; it's about giving them the tools to build a sustainable financial foundation through what I call the **Wealth Infinity Cycle**.

Teaching kids about the power of compounding early on is one of the greatest gifts parents can give. By helping them understand that even small savings, if consistently reinvested, can grow into substantial amounts, children can develop a long-term perspective on money. **The magic of compounding teaches kids** the importance of patience, discipline, and consistency –principles that will serve them well throughout their lives.

## The Wealth Infinity Cycle: A Lifelong Journey

The **Wealth Infinity Cycle** is the core principle of this book. It's a framework that shows how small habits, when built consistently, lead to lifelong skills, which can be monetised and reinvested, creating a cycle of compounding wealth.

The **Wealth Infinity Cycle** is built on three essential principles, or the **3 C's:**

1. **Commitment:** The journey to financial independence begins with commitment – committing to habits that will grow over time, whether it's saving a small portion of pocket money or learning new skills like coding, public speaking, or playing a musical instrument.

2. **Consistency:** Building wealth doesn't happen overnight. It requires consistently practising these habits and skills until they become second nature. Consistency is the bridge between effort and mastery, whether in managing money or developing skills that can be monetised in the future.

3. **Compounding:** Compounding is the secret ingredient to wealth-building. Just as compounding interest allows savings to grow exponentially, compounding skills and reinvesting passive income enable wealth to snowball over time. By teaching kids to reinvest their money and continually improve their skills, we help them build a cycle of continuous growth.

## The Role of Parents and Teachers

As parents and educators, we play a crucial role in guiding children through this journey. We need to teach them that wealth isn't just about earning money today but about making smart, long-term decisions that lead to financial independence. This book provides actionable steps for building that foundation. From forming small saving habits to encouraging children to explore their talents and build valuable skills, we can help kids create an asset base that will support them throughout their lives.

Our goal is to guide children until they reach a point where their **passive income exceeds their active income** – where their assets are generating enough returns to cover their needs and wants. At that point, the Wealth Infinity Cycle will run on its own, with little need for external support.

## What This Book Will Teach

This book will walk you through the process of helping children build their first portfolio and set the stage for lifelong financial success. It's not just about choosing stocks or setting up a savings account. It's about fostering a mindset of financial discipline, teaching children to value consistent effort, and showing them how to leverage the skills they develop into future wealth.

We'll cover topics such as:

- How to help children form early saving and investing habits.

- The importance of developing monetizable skills (beyond financial habits) and how to guide kids in exploring their interests.

- Teaching the concept of passive income and how it differs from active income.

- Understanding the power of compounding and how to reinvest earnings to grow wealth.

- Helping children set financial goals that go beyond short-term wants and focus on long-term financial independence.

## The Journey Starts Now

The journey to financial independence doesn't begin with a huge investment or a complex financial strategy. It starts with small, consistent actions taken every day. By committing to these actions and guiding our children in developing the right habits and skills, we give them the greatest gift of all – control over their financial future.

As we dive into this book, remember that financial success isn't just about money. It's about building a life where your skills, passions, and resources compound to create lasting security and freedom. And it all starts with the first step: helping kids build their first portfolio.

# Part 1

# Foundations of Financial Literacy

"The seeds of wealth are sown in small acts of
consistency, nurtured by discipline,
and harvested over a lifetime."

— Talanki Naveen Kumar Guptha

# Chapter 1

# The Power of Habits and Saving Early

## Introduction

From a young age, we are shaped by the habits we develop, and these habits play a critical role in our financial success. One of the most powerful lessons that can be instilled in children is the importance of saving early. Saving doesn't need to start big – it begins with small steps that form the foundation for a lifetime of financial discipline and success.

## My Story: The 5-Rupee Coin Habit

I remember the first time I was given the responsibility of going to the market to buy groceries. I was young, probably around 10 or 11 years old. My parents would give me money for groceries, and whatever change was left, often in the form of 5-rupee coins, was mine to keep. Since 5-rupee coins were not always easy to find, my parents encouraged me to save them whenever I received one. It didn't seem like much at the time, but every trip to the market was an opportunity to collect a small treasure.

At first, I didn't think much of these 5-rupee coins. They seemed insignificant. However over time, I developed a habit. I would take each coin and put it in a small box in my room. It wasn't long before the box started filling up. Little did I know, this simple habit was teaching me one of the most important financial lessons of my life: the power of saving consistently, no matter how small the amount. By the time the box was full, I had saved enough to buy something meaningful – a small cricket bat that I had wanted for months.

This habit of saving, formed at such a young age, stayed with me throughout my life. It taught me that no amount is too small to save and that discipline and consistency are the keys to financial growth.

## The Importance of Habits

Habits are powerful because they are automatic actions, ingrained in our behaviour. When you develop a habit like saving, you set yourself on a course for financial success without even thinking about it. As Charles Duhigg explains in *"The Power of Habit,"* habits are formed by a loop, which consists of a cue, a routine, and a reward. In my case, the cue was receiving the 5-rupee coins, the routine was putting them in the box, and the reward was seeing the box fill up over time.

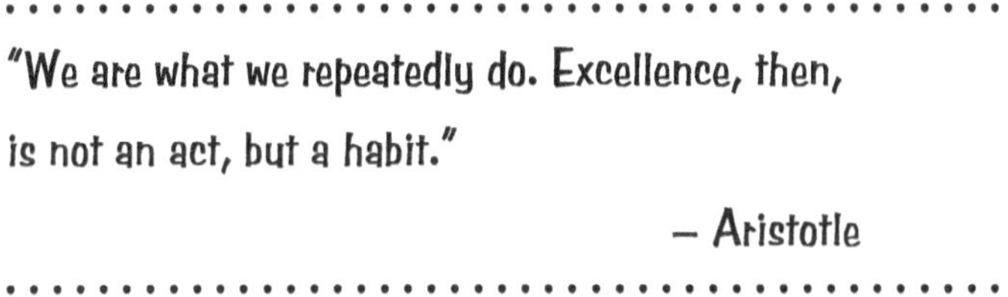


In the same way, developing a habit of saving early can lead to significant results over time. The habit doesn't have to start with large amounts of money – it can be as small as saving the spare change, just like I did with those 5-rupee coins.

## Why Starting Early Matters

When you start saving early, even if it's a small amount, you give your money more time to grow. The earlier you start, the longer your money can compound, and the more you'll have in the long run. This is why teaching kids the habit of saving at a young age is crucial. It's not about the amount; it's about the process and the mindset.

## The Magic of Starting Early: Why Time is Your Greatest Wealth Builder

Have you ever wished you could multiply your money while sleeping? That's not just a dream – it's the reality of starting your investment journey early. In this chapter, we'll explore why time is the most powerful tool in your investment arsenal and how starting early can transform modest savings into substantial wealth.

## The Tale of Two Investors

Meet Rahul and Priya, two individuals with different approaches to investing. Their stories perfectly illustrate the incredible power of time in wealth-building.

Rahul, a 15-year-old student, begins investing ₹500 monthly the money he saves from his pocket allowance. This might seem like a small amount, barely enough for a weekend movie and popcorn. Meanwhile, Priya, a 30-year-old professional, invests ₹1,000 monthly, double what Rahul puts aside.

Let's fast forward to when they both reach 60:

- Rahul's modest ₹500 monthly investment (total ₹2,70,000) grows to an impressive ₹25.30 lakh

- Priya's larger ₹1,000 monthly investment (total ₹3,60,000) reaches ₹15 lakh only.

The surprising outcome shows that despite investing less money each month, Rahul ends up with ₹10.30 lakh more than Priya. This isn't magic – it's the power of time.

## Understanding the Time Advantage

Think of investing like planting a mango tree. The earlier you plant it, the more seasons of fruit you'll enjoy. Similarly, every year of early investing is another year your money can grow and compound. Here's how different starting ages impact your wealth creation journey (assuming an 8% annual return and ₹1,000 monthly investment until age 60):

| Starting Age | Years Invested | Total Investment | Final Amount |
|---|---|---|---|
| 20 years | 40 years | ₹4.8 lakhs | ₹35 lakhs |
| 30 years | 30 years | ₹3.6 lakhs | ₹15 lakhs |
| 40 years | 20 years | ₹2.4 lakhs | ₹6 lakhs |
| 50 years | 10 years | ₹1.2 lakhs | ₹2 lakhs |

# Why Early Starters Win

### 1. The Power of Compound Interest

Einstein allegedly called compound interest the "eighth wonder of the world." When you start early, your returns begin earning their own returns, creating a snowball effect of wealth generation. Your money works harder so you don't have to.

### 2. Lower Monthly Pressure

Starting early means you can invest smaller amounts to reach the same goals. Consider this: to accumulate ₹50 lakhs by age 60:

– Starting at age 20: requires ₹1,000/month

– Starting at age 40: requires ₹8,000/month

### 3. More Room for Recovery

Young investors have time on their side when facing market downturns. A 25-year-old can ride out market volatility over decades, while a 50-year-old has less time to recover from significant market dips.

Breaking the Common Excuses

"I don't earn enough to invest."

- Even small amounts compound significantly over time.

- Start with what you can; even ₹500 monthly makes a difference

"I'll start when I have more money."

- Waiting costs you your most valuable asset: time.

The best time to start was yesterday; the second best is today.

"I don't know enough about investing."

- Start with simple instruments like mutual funds.

- Your knowledge will grow alongside your investments.

## Action Steps for Young Investors

### 1. Start Now

- Begin with any amount you can consistently invest.

- Increase your investment as your income grows.

### 2. Automate Your Investments

- Set up automatic transfers on payday.

- Remove the temptation to spend first and invest later.

### 3. Choose Growth Over Immediate Returns

- Focus on long-term wealth-building.

- Reinvest your returns to maximise compounding.

### 4. Stay Consistent

- Regular small investments beat irregular large ones.

- Think of investing as a non-negotiable monthly expense.

## The Bottom Line

Time is the young investor's greatest advantage – an advantage that once lost, can never be regained. While it's never too late to start investing, starting early gives you an unbeatable head start in your wealth creation journey. Remember: it's not about timing the market; it's about time in the market.

Your future self will thank you for every month you start earlier. Begin your investment journey today, and let time work its magic on your wealth.

• • • • • • • • • • • • • • • • • • • • • • • • • • • • • • • • • • • • • • • • •

"The best time to plant a tree was 20 years ago.

The second best time is now."

— Chinese Proverb

• • • • • • • • • • • • • • • • • • • • • • • • • • • • • • • • • • • • • • • • •

## Case Study: Warren Buffett's Early Start

Warren Buffett, one of the greatest investors of all time, began his journey into investing at the age of 11. He purchased three shares of Cities Service Preferred for $38 per share. While he didn't make a huge fortune from that investment, the lesson he learned was invaluable. Buffett realised the power of patience and long-term thinking, something that has become the hallmark of his investing philosophy.

In his words:

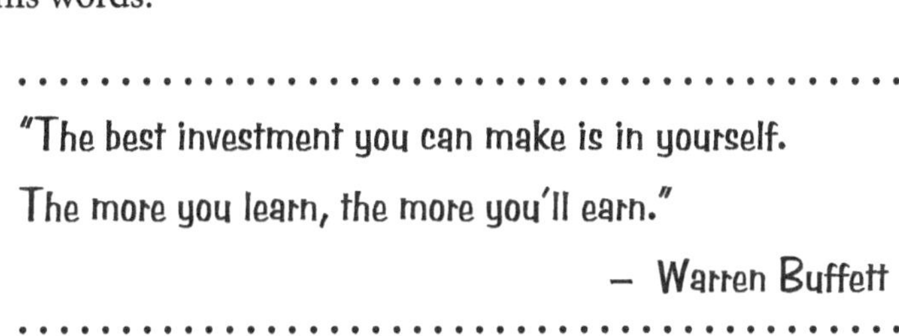


## Building a Habit of Saving in Children

So, how can we help children develop the habit of saving early? It starts with small steps, just like my experience with the 5-rupee coins. Here are some actionable tips for parents and educators to instil this habit in children:

1. **Provide Small Opportunities to Save**: Give your child a piggy bank or a designated box where they can store their savings. Encourage them to save a portion of their pocket money or any change they receive from purchases.

2. **Set Short-Term Goals**: Children often struggle with long-term thinking, so setting short-term goals can help them stay motivated. For example, if your child wants to buy a toy, help them figure out how much they need to save each week to reach that goal.

3. **Celebrate Milestones**: Recognise and celebrate when your child reaches a savings milestone. It could be something as simple as saving their first ₹100 or filling up their piggy bank. This reinforces the positive behaviour and makes them more likely to continue saving.

4. **Introduce the Concept of Interest**: Once your child has saved a small amount, introduce the idea of earning interest on their savings. You can do this by offering to "pay" them interest each week on the money they have saved.

## The Habit Loop: Saving, Investing, Reinvesting

The habit of saving early naturally leads to the next step – investing. Once children have developed the discipline to save consistently, they can begin learning about how to make their money work for them through investments. This is the foundation of the **Wealth Infinity Cycle**, which I will discuss further in later chapters.

The Wealth Infinity Cycle is based on three principles:

**1. Commitment**: The commitment to save and invest consistently.

**2. Consistency**: Regular contributions over time, no matter how small.

**3. Compounding**: Allowing your money to grow through the power of compound interest and reinvesting earnings.

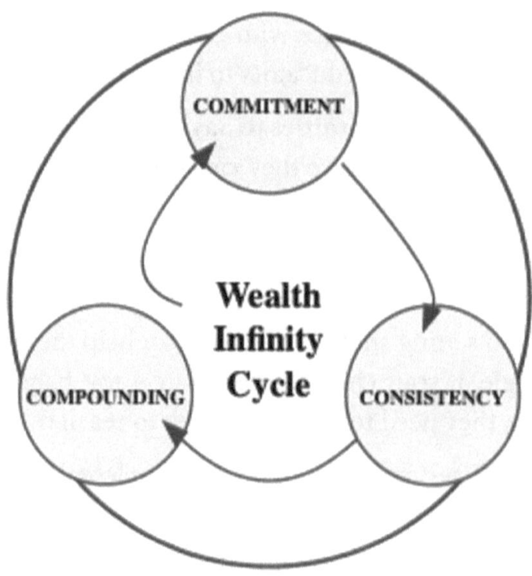

# C1 – Commitment: The Catalyst for an Early Start and Big Goals

Commitment is one of the most powerful tools you can harness on your journey toward financial success. Whether your goal is to build a modest portfolio or reach an ambitious target like ₹100 crores, commitment is what will separate you from those who give up or settle for mediocrity. It's not just about making a goal – it's about the unwavering dedication to achieve it, no matter the obstacles or the time it takes. In this chapter, we will explore the role of commitment in your financial journey, why people often fail to commit, and how you can cultivate it to ensure long-term success.

## Commitment as a Shift in Mindset

For many people, commitment is the missing link between where they are and where they want to be. Commitment is more than just setting a goal; it's a profound mindset shift. It's moving from a place of uncertainty—where you don't even have a specific goal—to a space where your goal becomes non-negotiable. It is this shift that transforms dreams into reality.

When you first decide to take control of your financial future, you might feel overwhelmed by how distant your target seems. If your goal is to achieve ₹100 crores, the task may feel impossible at the outset. But that's because most people fail to realise that significant achievements are the result of **small, consistent actions** compounded over time.

Commitment isn't about how fast you can achieve your goals; it's about staying dedicated to those goals no matter the pace. It's the realisation that **small things** make **big changes** in the long run. When you commit to financial growth, you understand that saving ₹100 today can lead to ₹1 crore or ₹100 crores in the future if you stay on track. This is the essence of the Wealth Infinity Cycle – your commitment to saving, investing, and reinvesting consistently leads to exponential growth.

## Awareness: The First Step Towards Commitment

Before commitment comes **awareness**. You can't commit to a goal if you're unaware of the potential benefits of doing so. Awareness is the starting point where you begin to realise that financial independence is achievable through discipline, consistency, and the power of compounding. Without awareness, many people drift through life without ever knowing that they have the power to change their financial destiny.

In his book *The Power of Now*, Eckhart Tolle emphasises that awareness is the foundation of any transformation. When you become aware of the possibilities that exist, you open yourself up to new ideas and opportunities. In the context of financial literacy, this awareness might come from understanding how the stock market works, how savings can grow through interest and compounding, or how financial discipline can create long-term wealth.

For example, if you're unaware of how compounding works, you might not see the value in saving small amounts of money regularly. But once you become aware of how even small savings can grow exponentially over time, you're more likely to commit to a savings plan. Awareness leads to a desire for change, which is the next step in this journey.

## Desire: The Fuel for Commitment

Once you become aware of the possibilities, the next step is **desire**. Desire is the emotional force that drives you towards your goals. It's what makes you want to take action. Without desire, awareness is pointless. Desire is what fuels your commitment – it's the reason behind why you want to achieve your financial goals.

In **Napoleon Hill's** *Think and Grow Rich*, he stresses that desire is the starting point of all achievement. No great success has ever been achieved without a burning desire behind it. For you, this might be the desire to achieve financial independence, to build a better future for your family, or to prove to yourself that you can reach a seemingly impossible goal, like ₹100 crores.

But desire alone isn't enough. Many people have the desire to succeed, yet they never get past the point of dreaming about it. They wish for better financial outcomes but don't take the necessary steps to achieve them. This is where **decision** comes into play.

## Decision: Turning Desire into Action

The third step in the commitment process is making a **decision**. This is where you take your desire and turn it into a firm resolution. A decision is a mental shift where you declare, "I am going to achieve this goal." Once you've made a decision, you cut off all other options. There's no going back, no more indecision, no more excuses. The decision solidifies your commitment.

In **Tony Robbins'** *Awaken the Giant Within*, he talks about the importance of decision-making as the turning point in any change process. Robbins states, "It is in your moments of decision that your destiny is shaped." The moment you decide to commit to your financial goals, your future starts to take shape.

It's important to note that making a decision doesn't mean you have all the answers or a perfectly clear path ahead. What it means is that you've committed to finding the way forward. Even if the journey is uncertain, you are resolved to continue until you reach your destination.

This decision to commit can apply to saving money, starting an investment portfolio, or sticking to a financial plan even when things get tough. Whether it's market volatility or unexpected expenses, the decision to stay committed means you don't abandon your goals at the first sign of difficulty.

## Commitment: The Key to Long-Term Success

Once you've made the decision, **commitment** naturally follows. Commitment is the dedication to seeing your goals through to the end, no matter what obstacles you face. It's about taking ownership of your decision and staying the course, even when progress seems slow or challenges arise.

In **Angela Duckworth's** *Grit*, commitment is a key component of grit, the combination of passion and perseverance toward long-term goals. Duckworth emphasises that while talent is important, it's commitment over time that leads to success. This is especially true in the world of finance. You don't need to be a financial genius to build wealth. What you need is commitment to stay the course, even when the journey gets tough or the rewards seem distant.

Commitment in financial growth means sticking to your saving and investment plans, even when you don't see immediate results. It means continuing to save small amounts, even when it feels like those amounts won't make a difference. Over time, those small contributions will compound and grow into something much larger. Commitment is about playing the long game and understanding that every small step matters.

## Why People Fail to Commit

Despite the importance of commitment, many people fail to fully commit to their financial goals. Why? Because they don't recognise the power of small actions. They mistakenly believe that achieving big goals requires big actions. As a result, they become discouraged when their initial efforts seem insignificant.

People often give up on their financial goals because they expect quick results. They might start saving or investing, but when they don't see immediate growth, they lose motivation and quit. This is a classic mistake. Financial growth, like any worthwhile goal, takes time. The key to success is not in dramatic, one-time efforts but in small, consistent actions taken over time.

Another reason people fail to commit is the fear of long-term responsibility. Commitment implies that you are in it for the long haul. For some, the idea of having to save or invest consistently for years or even decades feels overwhelming. But this fear of commitment is precisely what holds people back from achieving their financial goals.

## The Components of True Commitment

True commitment is built on several core components. These elements help ensure that once you commit to a goal, you have the foundation necessary to follow through.

1. **Awareness:** As mentioned earlier, awareness is the first step towards commitment. You need to be aware of your financial situation, your potential for growth, and the steps necessary to achieve your goals.

2. **Desire**: Desire is the emotional fuel that drives commitment. Without a strong desire to achieve your goals, commitment will fade in the face of challenges.

3. **Decision**: A firm decision is what solidifies your commitment. When you make a decision, you cut off all other options and dedicate yourself to the path ahead.

4. **Ownership**: Commitment means taking full responsibility for your actions and decisions. You own your financial future, and that ownership drives you to stay committed, no matter what happens.

5. **Resilience**: Commitment requires resilience. There will be setbacks along the way, but your commitment helps you bounce back and keep going, even when things get tough.

6. **Persistence**: Persistence is the willingness to stick with your goals, even when progress is slow. It's about showing up every day, making small contributions, and trusting that over time, those contributions will add up to something significant.

## Commitment from a Higher Perspective: Insights from Thought Leaders

Throughout history, commitment has been emphasised by great thinkers and leaders as the cornerstone of success. In *The 7 Habits of Highly Effective People*, Stephen Covey talks about the importance of commitment as part of being proactive. He suggests that commitment is a matter of principle, something you do because it's the right thing, not because it's easy or convenient. Covey's view reinforces the idea that commitment is rooted in deep values, such as financial responsibility, integrity, and long-term thinking.

In *Atomic Habits* by **James Clear,** commitment is viewed from the perspective of identity. Clear argues that commitment is not just about achieving a goal but about becoming the kind of person who naturally achieves that goal. For instance, if your goal is to build a substantial financial portfolio, you need to commit to becoming someone who makes smart financial decisions consistently. This means your commitment is tied not just to the end result but to the habits and identity you develop along the way.

## Commitment as a Lifelong Process

Commitment doesn't end once you achieve your financial goal. In fact, true commitment is a **lifelong process**. After you've reached your initial goals, new ones will emerge. For example, after building your first ₹1 crore portfolio, you might set your sights on ₹10 crore or even ₹100 crore. Each new goal requires the same level of commitment, discipline, and persistence as the first.

Financial success is not a destination but a continuous journey. By committing to your financial growth, you embrace a mindset that keeps you moving forward, no matter where you are on your journey. Commitment is the foundation of the Wealth Infinity Cycle, ensuring that as you grow, you continue to reinvest your wealth and stay dedicated to your goals for the long-term.

## Conclusion: Commitment is the Key to Unlocking Your Financial Future

In summary, commitment is the catalyst for achieving your financial goals. It transforms awareness into action, desire into discipline, and decisions into results. Without commitment, even the best financial plans will fall short. But with commitment, even the most ambitious goals—like building a ₹100 crore portfolio—are within reach.

Commitment isn't just about the big moments. It's about staying dedicated to the small, daily actions that lead to big results over time. By understanding the power of commitment, you can set yourself on the path to financial success and build the wealth and freedom you've always dreamed of.

## The Roadmap to 100 Crores: A Mindset for Lifelong Wealth

When teaching kids about saving and investing, it's essential to help them understand that even small actions today can lead to significant wealth over time. One way to illustrate this is through the **Roadmap to 100 Crores**, a long-term vision built on the foundation of **consistency** and **compounding**. The first milestone on this journey is to accumulate **₹10 lakh** by building strong financial habits early on.

## The Rule of 72: Understanding How Wealth Doubles

The **rule of 72** is a simple way to explain how long it takes for an investment to double at a given rate of return. You divide **72 by the rate of return** to estimate how many years it will take to double your money.

For example:

- At a **25% annual return**, your money doubles in **roughly 3 years** (72 ÷ 25 = 2.88, or about 3 years).

- At a **15% annual return**, it doubles in **around 4.8 years**.

- At a **10% annual return**, it doubles in **about 7.2 years**.

Now imagine consistently doubling your capital every 3 years for 30 years. Even starting with ₹10 lakh, through the power of compounding and consistency, this can grow into substantial wealth.

## Step 1: The Goal of Accumulating ₹10 Lakh

To achieve a bigger financial goal, you first need to build a **solid foundation**. For kids, the initial target should be to **accumulate ₹10 lakh** through disciplined saving and investing habits. Reaching this milestone gives them a **strong asset base** from which to compound further growth. The idea is to start early, with small amounts, and let their savings grow over time through consistent reinvestment.

By consistently saving, investing, and reinvesting, kids can see how their efforts compound into substantial amounts. This initial ₹10 lakh becomes the foundation for their **Roadmap to 100 Crores**.

## Step 2: Doubling Your Capital Every 3 Years for 30 Years

Once the ₹10 lakh asset base is accumulated, the next step is to grow this capital through disciplined investing. With a **25% annual return**, the investment will **double every 3 years**, and over 30 years, it can grow to incredible levels. Let's break this down:

1. **Start with ₹10 lakh**: With a 25% return, your capital doubles approximately every 3 years.

2. **Doubling every 3 years**:

   - Year 3: ₹10 lakh → ₹20 lakh

   - Year 6: ₹20 lakh → ₹40 lakh

   - Year 9: ₹40 lakh → ₹80 lakh

   - Year 12: ₹80 lakh → ₹1.6 crore

   - Year 15: ₹1.6 crore → ₹3.2 crore

   - Year 18: ₹3.2 crore → ₹6.4 crore

   - Year 21: ₹6.4 crore → ₹12.8 crore

   - Year 24: ₹12.8 crore → ₹25.6 crore

   - Year 27: ₹25.6 crore → ₹51.2 crore

   - **Year 30: ₹51.2 crore → ₹102.4 crore**

This shows how the **₹10 lakh initial capital** can grow into ₹100 crore over time, using the power of **compounding**.

## Reaching a 25% Return: The Challenge and the Strategy

While **Nifty 50 Index ETFs** provide **13% to 16% annual returns** over the long-term, achieving a **25% return** requires a more proactive approach. This is where **strategic investing** comes into play. In my upcoming book, I'll explain how to generate the **extra return** needed to reach the 25% level through methods such as:

- **Strategic stock selection**: Focusing on high-growth companies.

- **Capital turnover**: Reinvesting profits more frequently.

- **Risk management**: Balancing risk to maximise return.

## Teaching Kids the Power of Big Ambitions

By introducing children to the concept of **compounding** and the **rule of 72** early in life, we help them understand how even modest savings, when invested consistently, can grow into large sums over time.

Teaching kids to **aim for big goals**, like building their first ₹10 lakh, instills in them the **mindset of ambition** and shows them that financial success starts with small habits. The ultimate goal, however, is to take these initial savings and, through long-term investing, eventually achieve much larger financial targets like ₹100 crore. This is the **Roadmap to 100 Crores** – a path that begins with small, consistent actions and leads to significant wealth.

## Building Habits Towards Bigger Goals

As parents and educators, it's important to encourage kids to **build saving and investing habits** early in life. The **Roadmap to 100 Crores** serves as a motivational framework that instills **discipline, patience, and long-term thinking**. Starting with small savings and consistently reinvesting helps kids build their first ₹10 lakh – a goal that gives them the asset base to grow their wealth further.

By introducing kids to the **concept of compounding** and showing them how ₹10 lakh can grow into ₹100 crore over time, you teach them that **small actions today lead to big results tomorrow**. This way, kids not only learn the value of saving but also see the **potential of their investments to grow exponentially**.

## Personal Prompts

- "What's one thing you could save for right now? Could you start today?"
- "Is there something small you could start saving from your allowance or pocket money? Imagine what that might become in a year from now."

## Conclusion: The Power of Small Actions

It's important to remember that every financial success story begins with small, consistent actions. Whether it's saving 5-rupee coins or contributing to an investment account, the key is to start. By developing the habit of saving early, children can set themselves up for a lifetime of financial growth and success.

The takeaway here is simple: saving isn't just about the money; it's about building a habit. And when that habit is paired with discipline and long-term thinking, it becomes a powerful force for wealth creation.

## Reflection

"Think about the last time you saved for something important. How did it feel when you finally reached your goal?"

"Have you ever wanted something so much that you couldn't wait? What if you could wait and have twice as much later?"

## Key Takeaway Box

- Start small, but start early.

- Develop the habit of saving, no matter the amount.

- Consistency and discipline are the keys to long-term financial success.

# Chapter 2

# Understanding Money:
# From Pocket Money to Wealth-Building

## Introduction

Understanding the value of money is crucial for any financial journey. Most children are first introduced to the concept of money through pocket money – small amounts given by parents for daily expenses, treats, or rewards for good behaviour. While it may seem insignificant, pocket money serves as the foundation for learning key financial principles like earning, saving, and budgeting. In this chapter, we will explore how to teach kids the value of money, guide them in managing it wisely, and show them how these small lessons can evolve into wealth-building habits over time.

## My Story: Lessons from Pocket Money

Growing up, my first encounter with money management came from the pocket money I received. At first, like most children, I spent it impulsively on small treats – chocolates, comics, or little toys. But as time passed, I realised that if I wanted to save for something bigger and more meaningful, like a cricket bat or a video game, I needed to plan and manage my money better.

I remember the day I set my sights on buying a particular toy I had seen in a store. I didn't have enough money at that moment, so I decided to save a portion of my pocket money each week. It was a slow process, but eventually, I saved enough to buy it. The sense of achievement I felt taught me a valuable lesson: patience and planning are essential to managing money effectively. This small experience laid the foundation for my understanding of wealth-building.

## Teaching the Basics of Money to Children

Understanding money is about more than just having it – it's about knowing how to earn it, save it, and use it responsibly. The key is to start early, introducing children to concepts that are simple yet impactful. Here's how parents can guide their children in developing these skills:

1. **Earning Money**: For children, the concept of earning money often begins with pocket money or allowances. However, it's important to teach them that money is earned through effort. You can encourage this by tying pocket money to simple tasks, such as helping with household chores or completing assignments. This teaches children that money has value and is a reward for hard work.

2. **Saving Money**: The idea of saving should be introduced right alongside the concept of earning. One of the most effective methods is to encourage children to set aside a portion of their pocket money for savings. This can be in the form of a piggy bank, a savings jar, or even a simple savings account if they are old enough.

3. **Spending Money**: While saving is essential, it's equally important for children to understand how to spend wisely. Teach them to prioritise their needs over wants. For example, if they're saving for a larger goal, encourage them to avoid impulsive purchases and think carefully before spending.

4. **Budgeting**: A basic budget helps children visualise their money and how it can be allocated towards different goals. Creating a simple budget with columns for saving, spending, and giving can help children learn to plan their finances.

## Example: The Power of Budgeting

Let's say a child receives ₹500 as pocket money each month. With the guidance of a parent, they create a simple budget:

- ₹250 goes into savings (for a long-term goal like buying a new bicycle).

- ₹200 is set aside for spending (on small items like snacks or toys).

- ₹50 is allocated for giving (to a charity or to help someone in need).

This basic structure helps the child understand how to manage their limited resources wisely. Over time, as they see their savings grow and their spending becomes more purposeful, they start to build a positive relationship with money.

## How Small Actions Lead to Wealth-Building

The simple act of managing pocket money effectively sets the foundation for wealth-building. Just as I learned through my experience of saving for a toy, children who are taught to save and budget from an early age develop habits that will serve them well in adulthood. These small habits, when compounded over time, can lead to significant wealth accumulation.

> "It's not how much money you make, but how much money you keep, how hard it works for you, and how many generations you keep it for."
>
> — Robert Kiyosaki, author of Rich Dad Poor Dad

## Wealth-Building Through Goal-Setting

Another critical aspect of understanding money is teaching children how to set financial goals. Whether it's saving for a toy, a trip, or a future education fund, goals provide direction and motivation. Here's how parents can guide children in setting goals that promote wealth-building:

1. **Short-Term Goals**: These are smaller goals that can be achieved within a few weeks or months. For example, saving for a toy or a special outing. Short-term goals teach children that saving leads to rewards.

2. **Long-Term Goals**: These are larger goals that require more time and effort to achieve, such as saving for a new bicycle, a trip, or even contributing to a future college fund. Long-term goals teach patience, discipline, and the power of delayed gratification.

By breaking down financial goals into short-term and long-term categories, children can learn to plan and prioritise their spending and saving effectively.

## Case Study: Rakesh Jhunjhunwala's First Investment

Let's take a look at the story of Indian investor Rakesh Jhunjhunwala, often referred to as India's Warren Buffett. Jhunjhunwala's first introduction to money and investing came from his father, who was a financial professional. However, it wasn't his father who gave him his first stock market tip – it was his own curiosity and discipline that led him to success.

Jhunjhunwala started small, investing the money he had saved over time. His first significant purchase was in Tata Tea, and it paid off handsomely. Jhunjhunwala's discipline in reinvesting his profits and learning from his mistakes helped him become one of the wealthiest and most respected investors in India. His story teaches us that wealth-building is about more than just luck – it's about patience, consistency, and understanding how to manage money wisely.

## The Psychology of Money: Why It Matters

Understanding money is not just about the numbers; it's about developing the right mindset. Many adults struggle with financial management because they were never taught to think about money the right way. By instilling the right psychology in children early on, we can set them up for a lifetime of financial success. Here are a few key psychological principles to teach:

- **Delayed Gratification**: The ability to wait for a reward is one of the most important skills for wealth-building. Children who learn to delay gratification are more likely to be successful in saving and investing.

- **Emotional Detachment from Money**: Money can be a source of stress, especially when it's linked to emotions. Teaching children to view money as a tool, rather than something to be emotionally attached to, can help them make more rational financial decisions in the future.

- **Positive Reinforcement**: Celebrate financial milestones, no matter how small. Positive reinforcement encourages children to continue making good financial decisions.

## Creating a Financial Blueprint

To help children take their understanding of money further, parents can guide them in creating a financial blueprint. This is a simple plan that outlines their earning, saving, and spending goals. Here's a step-by-step process:

1. **Identify Income Sources**: Start by identifying where money comes from. This could be pocket money, gifts, or earnings from small jobs.

2. **Set Saving Goals**: Establish specific saving goals, both short-term and long-term.

3. **Track Spending**: Encourage children to keep a record of their spending. This helps them understand where their money is going and how they can adjust their budget.

4. **Review and Adjust**: Periodically review the blueprint to see if any adjustments are needed. As children grow and their financial needs change, their blueprint should evolve as well.

## Conclusion: Building a Healthy Relationship with Money

The journey from pocket money to wealth-building begins with understanding the basics of earning, saving, and budgeting. By teaching children how to manage their money wisely from a young age, we set them up for a lifetime of financial independence. These lessons may start small, but their impact will grow over time, helping children develop healthy habits that lead to wealth creation.

## Key Takeaway Box

- Teach children the value of money through earning, saving, and budgeting.

- Help them set short-term and long-term financial goals.

- Foster the right mindset by focusing on delayed gratification and positive reinforcement.

# Chapter 3

# Why Financial Discipline Matters

## Introduction

Financial discipline is the cornerstone of financial success. Without it, even the most well-planned budget can fall apart. While the word "discipline" might sound strict or challenging, in the realm of personal finance, it simply refers to the ability to stick to your financial goals, manage your money wisely, and avoid unnecessary debt. The concept of discipline is essential not just for adults but also for children, as it forms the foundation of long-term financial health.

In this chapter, we'll explore what financial discipline means, why it's important, and how teaching kids about discipline at an early age can set them up for a lifetime of success. This chapter also ties into the broader theme of the **Wealth Infinity Cycle** – a cycle that relies on disciplined saving, investing, and reinvesting for continual growth.

Growing up, I often admired my grandfather's financial habits. He was someone who understood the value of every rupee and rarely spent money impulsively. He would always tell me, "If you don't need it, don't buy it. But if you do need it, make sure you've saved for it."

I remember wanting a new video game console, which was quite expensive at the time. My grandfather sat me down and explained the concept of saving gradually, bit by bit, instead of asking for the money all at once. He suggested that I save part of my pocket money each week, no matter how small the amount. It felt frustrating at first because I wanted the console immediately, but over time, I noticed my savings were growing. Eventually, I saved enough to buy the console myself.

The lesson here wasn't just about saving for a toy. It was about learning the value of patience and how discipline can lead to achieving long-term goals. This early experience with disciplined saving helped shape my understanding of money management, and it's something I still carry with me today.

## What is Financial Discipline?

Financial discipline is the ability to control your spending and saving habits in a way that aligns with your financial goals. For adults, this might mean budgeting effectively, avoiding unnecessary debt, and saving for retirement. For kids, financial discipline might look like saving a part of their pocket money, waiting to make a purchase until they've saved enough, or learning to differentiate between needs and wants.

The principles of financial discipline are simple yet powerful:

1. Plan and set goals.

2. Spend within your means.

3. Prioritise saving and investing.

4. Avoid impulsive decisions.

5. Stick to your plan even when tempted.

Mastering these habits from a young age can make all the difference in achieving financial success later in life.

## The Importance of Discipline in Financial Growth

Why is financial discipline so important? The answer lies in the concept of **compound growth**. The earlier you start saving, the more time your money has to grow. This is the heart of the **Wealth Infinity Cycle**, a disciplined, consistent approach to managing your money that results in continuous growth.

When kids are disciplined with their money, they're not just saving for short-term goals like toys or games. They're building habits that will serve them well into adulthood. Here's why discipline matters:

- **Consistency is key**: Small, regular savings add up over time. A disciplined saver will accumulate more wealth than someone who saves sporadically or impulsively.

- **Long-term thinking**: Financial discipline teaches kids to think beyond immediate gratification. Instead of spending their money as soon as they receive it, disciplined kids learn to save for bigger, more meaningful goals.

- **Better decision-making**: With financial discipline comes the ability to make better financial decisions. Kids who learn to be disciplined with money are less likely to make impulsive purchases and more likely to weigh their options carefully.

. . . . . . . . . . . . . . . . . . . . . . . . . . . . . . . . . . . . . . . . . . .

*"The art is not in making money, but in keeping it."*

*— Proverb*

. . . . . . . . . . . . . . . . . . . . . . . . . . . . . . . . . . . . . . . . . . .

## The Wealth Infinity Cycle and Discipline

The concept of financial discipline ties directly into the **Wealth Infinity Cycle,** the process of saving, investing, and reinvesting to create continuous financial growth. Each phase of this cycle requires discipline.

- **Saving**: It takes discipline to save a portion of your income regularly. For kids, this might mean setting aside part of their pocket money or earnings from chores. By teaching them the habit of saving early, you set them up to always think about their future before making spending decisions.

- **Investing**: Once kids have saved enough, the next step in the Wealth Infinity Cycle is investing. But here's the catch – investing is not a get-rich-quick strategy. It requires discipline to choose investments wisely and avoid making rash decisions based on fear or greed.

- **Reinvesting**: The final step in the cycle is reinvesting your gains to grow your wealth even further. This step is crucial but often neglected. Disciplined investors understand the power of compounding, and instead of spending their returns, they reinvest them for even greater long-term growth.

## Understanding the Consequences of Poor Discipline

Without discipline, even the best financial plans can crumble. For example, if a child receives ₹500 as pocket money and spends it all on candy or toys without saving any, they won't have anything left for more meaningful purchases later on. This lack of discipline can extend into adulthood, where impulsive spending can lead to debt, financial stress, and a lack of savings.

Here's a real-life example: many adults struggle with credit card debt because they spend more than they earn. Without discipline, it's easy to accumulate debt and fall into a cycle of financial hardship. This is why it's so important to teach kids discipline from an early age – they'll be less likely to make the same mistakes when they grow older.

## Case Study: The Tale of Two Savers

Let's take a look at two imaginary children: Ravi and Vritika.

- **Ravi** receives ₹500 each month as pocket money. He loves spending it on toys, snacks, and games. By the end of the month, he has nothing left in his piggy bank.

- **Vritika** also receives ₹500 each month, but she has learned the value of discipline. Every month, she sets aside ₹200 into her savings jar. After one year, Vritika has ₹2,400 saved up, while Ravi has nothing.

The difference between Ravi and Vritika is simple: discipline. Vritika's small but consistent savings habit allowed her to accumulate a significant amount of money over time, while Ravi's lack of discipline left him with nothing to show for his spending.

This example illustrates that financial success isn't just about how much money you earn – it's about how you manage it.

## Practical Tips for Teaching Financial Discipline

1. **Set Clear Goals**: Help your child set clear, achievable financial goals. This could be saving up for a special toy, a family trip, or even their future education. Having a goal gives children a sense of purpose and makes it easier for them to stick to their saving plan.

2. **Create a Savings Plan**: Work with your child to create a savings plan. Encourage them to save a specific percentage of their pocket money each week. You can even use a simple chart to track their progress and celebrate milestones along the way.

3. **Reward Discipline**: Positive reinforcement goes a long way. If your child reaches a savings goal, consider rewarding them with a small bonus or an additional privilege. This will reinforce the value of discipline and encourage them to keep going.

4. **Introduce the Envelope System**: This is a fun and effective way to teach kids about budgeting. Give them three envelopes: one for saving, one for spending, and one for giving. Each time they receive money, they divide it between the three envelopes. This helps them visualise where their money is going and teaches them the importance of balancing their priorities.

5. **Model Discipline**: Children learn by example. Show your kids that you practice financial discipline in your own life. Share stories of how you save for bigger goals and avoid impulsive purchases.

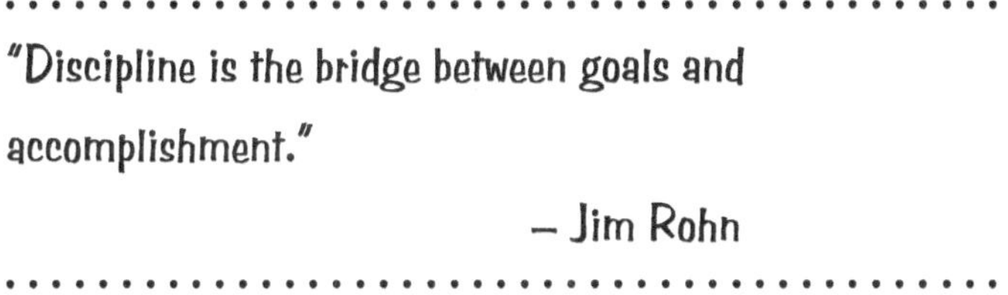


## Case Study: Steve Jobs and Financial Focus

Steve Jobs, the co-founder of Apple, was known for his laser-like focus on his goals. In the early days of Apple, he and his co-founder Steve Wozniak were both deeply committed to building a successful company, and that required discipline. Jobs was meticulous about how Apple spent its money, and he focused on reinvesting profits back into the business to fuel growth.

This same mindset applies to personal finance. Financial discipline is about focusing on your long-term goals and being careful with how you manage your resources. By teaching kids to approach their finances with the same focus, you're helping them lay the groundwork for future success.

# C2 – Consistency as the Cornerstone of Financial Growth

## Consistency in Financial Growth

Consistency in finance is about developing and maintaining sustainable habits that support long-term goals. In the Wealth Infinity Cycle, consistency fuels incremental growth, which, over time, compounds into significant wealth. It transforms isolated financial actions, like saving and investing, into a powerful cycle of growth.

### The Role of Consistency in the Wealth Infinity Cycle

- **Commitment to Regular Actions**: Consistency bridges the gap between initial commitment and eventual compounding. By sticking to a regular pattern of saving, budgeting, or investing, children and young learners can see how even small, steady efforts create a larger impact.

- **Sustainability and Flexibility**: Unlike rigid discipline, consistency is adaptable. If life events interrupt progress, the journey can resume without starting from scratch. For instance, if an unexpected expense disrupts savings for a month, the habit can restart easily, demonstrating resilience.

### Understanding the Difference: Discipline vs. Consistency vs. Practice

- **Discipline**: Involves following rules or making a conscious decision to prioritise goals. Discipline is often strict and focused on immediate control over actions.

- **Consistency**: Involves sustaining routines over time. It's flexible and maintains momentum even with occasional pauses, making it easier to resume after breaks.

- **Practice**: Repeating actions to improve skill or understanding. Practice helps to reinforce both discipline and consistency, building comfort and confidence with financial habits.

| Aspect | Discipline | Consistency | Practice |
|---|---|---|---|
| **Focus** | Following rules and regulations | Maintaining regular patterns | Repetition to improve |
| **Nature** | Rigid, structured | Flexible, sustainable | Adaptive, skill-building |
| **Motivation** | External enforcement | Internal commitment | Internal drive to improve |
| **Time Frame** | Short-term adherence | Long-term habits | Long-term skill development |
| **Recovery** | Harder to recover after breaks | Easier to resume after pauses. | Builds resilience through repetition. |

## Strategic Patience in Consistency

- **Understanding Strategic Patience**: Strategic patience is the ability to stick to a financial plan even when immediate results are not visible. This aligns with the Wealth Infinity Cycle, as the compounding effects of consistency require time and steady input.

- **Importance in Financial Growth**: Rather than expecting instant returns, learners should understand that wealth-building is a gradual process. For instance, contributing to a savings account regularly may seem slow initially, but the balance builds momentum over time.

- **Example**: Showcasing an illustration of a young investor who consistently invests a small amount each month in an ETFs. Initially, the growth appears slow, but with patience, the investments grow exponentially.

## Consistency as Practice: Building Financial Skills Over Time

- **Learning and Practising Basics**: Practice involves understanding financial tools, practising budgeting, and reviewing savings goals regularly. Practice supports consistency by making the process enjoyable and builds confidence.

- **Resilience through Practice**: By practising these skills, learners can adjust to different financial conditions and continue with their financial plans.

- **Example**: Practising regular budgeting and making small adjustments as circumstances change teaches flexibility and increases financial confidence.

## Motivating Consistency: Tools and Tips for Staying the Course

- **Visualisation Tools**: Use charts and goal visualisations (like a savings tracker) to illustrate progress; even small steps add motivation to stay consistent.

- **Mini Goals and Rewards**: Celebrating minor milestones—such as reaching a savings milestone or achieving a set investment target—boosts morale and reinforces positive behaviour.

## Quotes for Inspiration

"Success is the sum of small efforts,

repeated day in and day out."

— Robert Collier

"In every job that must be done, there is an element of

fun. You find the fun, and—snap!—the job's a game."

— Mary Poppins

## Key Takeaways on Consistency in Wealth-Building

- Consistency enables sustainable growth in wealth and builds financial habits that are easier to maintain long-term.

- Strategic patience is essential; while results may take time, the compounded effect of regular actions yields substantial outcomes.

- Practising financial skills reinforces consistency, enabling resilience and flexibility in the face of challenges.

## Actionable Items

- **Start with a Savings Goal**: Help your child set a short-term savings goal and create a plan to achieve it.

- **Practice the Envelope System**: Introduce the three-envelope system to help your child manage their money.

- **Track Savings Together**: Use a savings chart to track progress and celebrate milestones.

- **Be a Role Model**: Lead by example – show your child how you practise financial discipline in your own life.

## Key Takeaways

- Financial discipline is essential for achieving long-term financial success.

- The Wealth Infinity Cycle relies on disciplined saving, investing, and reinvesting.

- Without discipline, even the best financial plans can fail.

- Teaching kids to set goals and stick to their savings plans will set them up for success in adulthood.

Financial discipline might not be the most exciting concept for kids, but it's one of the most important. By helping them develop these habits early, you're giving them a powerful tool that will serve them for the rest of their lives.

# Chapter 4

# Monetizing Habits – Turning Savings into Investment Capital

## Introduction

Wealth-building doesn't require starting with large sums of money. Instead, it begins with small, consistent actions that compound over time. The process is similar to planting a tree – starting with a seed and nurturing it over time until it grows. In financial terms, this seed is your savings, and the way you nurture it is by turning it into investment capital.

In this chapter, we'll explore the idea of monetising habits – teaching kids how to convert their savings into investments, which in turn helps their money grow. We will also expand on the **Wealth Infinity Cycle**, emphasising that disciplined saving can lead to investments, and those investments can generate returns to save and reinvest. This continuous cycle is the key to long-term wealth-building.

## Meet Aarav

Aarav was a bright 12-year-old who loved his video games and outdoor sports. He wasn't particularly concerned with saving money. Every time his grandparents gave him some cash for his birthday, he spent it quickly on the latest gadgets or games.

But Aarav's parents wanted to teach him the importance of saving and investing. So one day, they introduced him to a simple idea: Instead of spending all his money, why not save part of it and see how it could grow? Aarav wasn't too interested at first, but his parents piqued his curiosity by showing him how investing works. They explained, "Just like planting a tree, if you put your money in the right place, it will grow over time."

Intrigued, Aarav agreed to try saving a little bit from his next allowance. By the time his birthday rolled around, Aarav had saved ₹2,000. His parents then helped him invest this money in a mutual fund, explaining that it was a safe place to start for a beginner like him. They showed him how, over time, his investment could earn returns, and those returns could be reinvested to make his money grow even more.

At first, Aarav was unsure. He didn't see immediate results. But after a few months, he noticed that his ₹2,000 had grown slightly – it wasn't a big amount, but it was more than what he had started with. This made him realise the power of investing. From that day on, Aarav made it a habit to save part of his pocket money each month and invest it. Slowly, his savings began to grow, and so did his understanding of money.

## The Power of Monetising Habits

Monetising habits means turning small, consistent actions—like saving—into something that can generate more value, such as investments. For kids, the habit of saving is an important first step, but it's only half the equation. To truly build wealth, they need to learn to invest their savings.

## Here's why monetising habits are so important

1. **Savings alone can't keep up with inflation.** If money is simply saved in a piggy bank or a low-interest account, its value can decrease over time due to inflation.

2. **Investing grows money.** When savings are invested wisely, they can grow and generate returns over time.

3. **Small contributions can lead to big growth.** Kids don't need to start with large amounts – regular small investments can accumulate and grow significantly.

Teaching kids to convert their savings into investments shows them that their money can work for them. Once they understand this concept, they can take the next step in the **Wealth Infinity Cycle** – reinvesting their returns to generate more wealth over time.

## How Aarav Learned to Turn Savings into Investments

After Aarav's parents introduced him to investing, they helped him take his first steps towards turning his savings into investment capital. Here's how it worked:

1. **Understanding Investing**: Aarav's parents explained that investing means using money to buy something that can grow in value over time – like stocks or mutual funds. For Aarav, they decided to start with a mutual fund, which was a safer option than individual stocks.

2. **Starting Small**: Aarav didn't have a lot of money saved up, but his ₹2,000 was enough to begin investing. His parents explained that even small amounts, when invested regularly, can grow significantly over time.

3. **Risk and Reward**: Aarav also learned that investing carries some risk, but with smart choices, he could reduce the chances of losing money. By choosing diversified investments like mutual funds, he could lower his risk while still giving his money a chance to grow.

4. **Making It a Habit**: Aarav made it a habit to save part of his pocket money and invest it. Every month, he would set aside a small amount and watch his savings grow through regular investments. This habit helped him understand that money isn't just for spending – it's also for growing.

> "The journey to wealth isn't a race; it's a process of building habits, learning, and nurturing the cycle of growth."
>
> — Talanki Naveen Kumar Guptha

## How to Convert Savings into Investment Capital

The next step for children, once they've learned the habit of saving, is to show them how to turn those savings into investments. Here's how you can guide kids through this process:

1. **Choose the Right Investment Vehicle**: For beginners like Aarav, starting with a mutual fund or an Index ETFs is a good option. These types of investments allow for diversification, which reduces risk.

2. **Open a Demat Account**: If the child is underage, you'll need to open a joint account or an account under parental supervision. Many platforms allow you to start investing with small amounts.

3. **Start Small**: Just like Aarav, kids can start with a small amount – ₹500 or ₹1,000. The goal is to help them understand the process and to build confidence

4. **Track the Investment**: Help kids track their investment's performance. This keeps them engaged and teaches them how investments work over time.

5. **Reinvest Returns**: Once the investment starts generating returns, teach kids to reinvest them. This is where the **Wealth Infinity Cycle** comes into play: saving, investing, and reinvesting the returns to maximise growth.

## Case Study: Aarav's Growing Wealth

As Aarav continued to save and invest, his small savings began to grow. Over the first year, Aarav's ₹2,000 investment earned him an additional ₹100. While it wasn't much at first, Aarav understood that his money was growing without any extra effort. He was excited to see his small habit of saving and investing start to pay off.

Encouraged by his early success, Aarav continued the habit of saving a portion of his pocket money and investing it in the mutual fund. Over the next few years, Aarav saw his investments grow steadily. The most important lesson he learned was that even a small habit, when paired with smart investing, can lead to big results over time.

## The Wealth Infinity Cycle: Turning Savings into Investments

The **Wealth Infinity Cycle** relies on disciplined saving, investing, and reinvesting. Aarav's experience demonstrates how saving just a little bit and investing it regularly can create a continuous cycle of wealth-building. The steps are simple:

- **Save regularly**: Set aside a portion of your money each time you receive it.

- **Invest those savings**: Once you have saved enough, invest in a diversified option like an Index ETFs or mutual fund.

- **Reinvest returns**: As your investment earns returns, reinvest them to keep the cycle going.

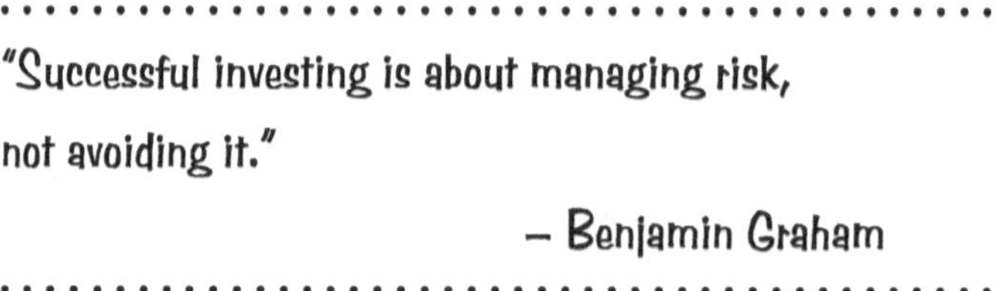


## Practical Tips for Teaching Kids to Monetise Their Habits

1. **Use Pocket Money as a Starting Point**: Encourage kids to save a portion of their pocket money. This can be the seed money for their first investment.

2. **Introduce Fun Investment Tools**: There are many child-friendly apps and tools that simulate real-life investing, helping kids get familiar with the process without risk.

3. **Set a Goal for Investment**: Help kids set a savings goal for when they can invest, such as saving ₹1,000 before they choose their first mutual fund or ETFs.

4. **Use Visuals to Explain Compounding**: Show kids how compounding works using simple charts or online calculators. Visual examples help them grasp how their money grows over time.

## Key Takeaways

Saving is the first step, but investing is where true wealth-building happens.

- Teaching kids to turn their savings into investment capital helps them understand how to grow their money over time.

- Small investments, when combined with the habit of saving, can lead to significant growth due to the power of compounding.

- The **Wealth Infinity Cycle** shows that consistent saving, investing, and reinvesting can create a lifelong pattern of financial growth.

By turning savings into investment capital, children like Aarav can learn early on that their money can work for them – setting the foundation for a financially successful future.

# Chapter 5

# Introduction to Investing: Demystifying Stocks and Index ETFs

Investing can seem intimidating, especially when you're just starting out. But if you take a closer look, it's not as complicated as it seems. Whether you are new to investing or just starting to learn, the idea of building wealth through stocks and ETFs is exciting because it brings you one step closer to financial independence.

This chapter will simplify these complex concepts, focusing on beginner-friendly investment options—**Index ETFs**—and setting the foundation for more advanced strategies in later chapters.

## The Power of Investing Early

Before we dive into specifics, let's address why investing early matters. The earlier you start investing, the more time you give your money to grow through the power of **compounding** – the third "C" in our **Wealth Infinity Cycle**. Compounding allows your returns to generate additional returns, which snowball over time.

**Example:** If you invest ₹10,000 at 12% annual return and leave it untouched, in 10 years it will grow to ₹31,058. In 20 years, it becomes ₹96,463, and in 30 years, it turns into a whopping ₹2,99,599. The key ingredient here is **time**, which magnifies the power of compounding.

## What Are Stocks and Index ETFs?

**Let's start with the basics:**

- **Stocks** represent ownership in a company. When you buy a stock, you own a small piece of that company. If the company grows, the value of your stock goes up, and you make money. But if the company faces losses, your stock value might go down.

- **Index ETFs** (Exchange-Traded Funds) are baskets of stocks that track a market index, like the **Nifty 50** or **Bank Nifty**. When you invest in an Index ETFs, you invest in a range of companies all at once. This reduces risk because you're not relying on a single company to do well.

## Why Start with Index ETFs?

Index ETFs are ideal for beginner investors for several reasons:

- **Diversification**: By holding a wide range of stocks, Index ETFs spread out your risk. If one company in the index does poorly, others may perform better, balancing things out.

- **Low-Cost**: Index ETFs typically have lower fees compared to mutual funds or other types of investments.

- **Steady Growth**: Historically, stock indices like Nifty 50 or Sensex have shown steady growth over the long-term.

**Key Takeaway**: Investing in Index ETFs is like buying the entire market. You're betting on the long-term growth of the economy rather than trying to pick individual winners. This strategy is less risky and a great starting point for young investors.

**Example:** Aarav's First Investment in Index ETFs

Aarav, a 16-year-old, saved up ₹5,000 and wanted to invest. Instead of buying individual stocks, which he found confusing, he started with an **Index ETFs** tracking the Nifty 50. He set up a plan to invest ₹1,000 each month. Over time, Aarav saw his small investments grow through the power of compounding and the steady rise of the overall market.

By staying committed to his plan, Aarav built a strong foundation for future investments. His choice of an Index ETFs allowed him to sleep well at night without worrying about the daily fluctuations of individual stocks.

## How to Choose the Right Index ETFs

Not all Index ETFs are created equal. Here's a simple checklist to help you decide:

**Index Selection**

- Choose well-established indices like Nifty 50 or Bank Nifty
- These contain top-performing companies across sectors
- Consider sector-specific indices based on your investment strategy
- Look for indices with proven long-term track records

**Expense Ratio**

- Lower is better (typically 0.05% to 0.50%)
- Directly impacts your returns
- Compare ratios among similar ETFs
- Even small differences compound over time

**Tracking Error**

- Measures how closely ETFs follows its index
- Lower tracking error (ideally below 0.5%) indicates better fund management
- Check consistency of tracking error over time
- Higher tracking error means the ETFs isn't replicating the index effectively

**Liquidity Factors**

- Trading Volume: Higher daily volumes mean easier buying/selling.
- Bid-Ask Spread: Smaller spread indicates better liquidity.
- Average Daily Trading Value: Higher values suggest better market acceptance.
- Look for at least 1000+ units traded daily.

**Fund Size (AUM)**

- Larger AUM generally means:

- ◦ Better stability
- ◦ Lower risk of fund closure
- ◦ More efficient trading
- Aim for ETFs with AUM above ₹100 crores.

**Historical Performance**

- Compare returns across different time periods
- Check performance during market ups and downs
- Look for consistency rather than just high returns
- Remember: past performance doesn't guarantee future results

**Market Maker Quality**

- Strong market makers ensure:
  - ◦ Consistent liquidity
  - ◦ Tighter bid-ask spreads
  - ◦ Better price efficiency
- Check authorised participants' reputation

**Hidden Costs**

- Brokerage fees
- Demat account charges
- Impact cost during large trades
- Tax implications

# Quotes to Inspire Your Journey

. . . . . . . . . . . . . . . . . . . . . . . . . . . . . . . . . . . . . . .

*"An investment in knowledge pays the best interest."*

— Benjamin Franklin

. . . . . . . . . . . . . . . . . . . . . . . . . . . . . . . . . . . . . . .

This quote reminds us that learning is the most powerful tool in investing. By educating yourself about different investment vehicles like **Index ETFs**, you are better prepared to make informed financial decisions.

## Key Takeaways

1. **Start Early**: The earlier you start investing, the more time your money has to grow through compounding.

2. **Index ETFs Are Beginner-Friendly**: They offer diversification, lower risk, and steady long-term growth, making them ideal for new investors.

3. **Commitment and Consistency**: Small, regular investments in Index ETFs, as demonstrated by Aarav, can lead to significant growth over time. Even if the stock market fluctuates, stay consistent with your investments.

4. **Compounding**: The real magic of wealth-building happens when your returns generate more returns. Be patient and let your investments compound over time.

## Call to Action: Start Small, Start Now

Take action today! You don't need a huge amount of money to begin your investing journey. Open a **demat** account with a brokerage platform that offers Index ETFs, set up an automatic monthly investment, and watch your wealth grow.

Even starting with ₹500 or ₹1,000 per month can make a big difference in the long run. The important thing is to get started and stay committed.

## Reflection: Your First Investment

Take a moment to reflect on how investing fits into your personal financial goals. Are you ready to commit to a long-term investment plan? What small steps can you take today to set yourself up for future success?

Write down your thoughts and answer these questions:

- What is the first step you'll take towards investing in Index ETFs?

- How much can you commit to investing each month?

- What long-term goals will these investments help you achieve?

## Summary: The Importance of Consistency in Investing

Investing is not about quick wins or trying to beat the market. It's about making steady, consistent contributions that grow over time. Index ETFs are a great way to start your investment journey because they provide broad market exposure with lower risk.

By understanding the basics of Index ETFs and the **power of consistent contributions**, you're already ahead of many others who are unsure where to begin. As you move forward, remember that the most important part of the Wealth Infinity Cycle is sticking with your investments, even when the market seems volatile. Stay focused, be consistent, and let compounding work its magic.

## Conclusion

With your foundation in saving and discipline already set, you are now ready to embrace the second "C" in the Wealth Infinity Cycle – **Consistency**. Continue your financial journey with small, regular investments in Index ETFs, and stay patient. In the next chapter, we will dive deeper into the incredible power of compounding, which will truly accelerate your wealth-building efforts.

# Chapter 6

# The Magic of Compounding – Time vs. Rate of Return

## Introduction C3 - Compounding as the multiplier of wealth

Compounding is a simple yet powerful financial concept that has transformed the lives of many successful investors over time. At its core, compounding means earning interest-on-interest, and it enables your savings to grow exponentially when given enough time. The earlier you start saving and investing, the more you stand to benefit from compounding. It is often said, "Money makes money, and the money that money makes, makes money." This chapter will delve into the components and dimensions of compounding—**rate of return, time, reinvestment**, and **consistency**—and demonstrate why time is the most crucial factor, especially for young investors. We will explore how famous personalities like Warren Buffett and Rakesh Jhunjhunwala used this principle to build their fortunes.

## The Components of Compounding: Rate of Return, Time, Reinvestment (turnover of capital), and Consistency

There are four major components that make compounding work:

1. **Rate of Return**: This refers to the percentage gain on your investment. A higher rate of return leads to faster compounding, but it also comes with higher risks. In the context of children or beginners, the goal should be to secure a modest return with lower risk – this is where instruments like **Index ETFs** shine.

2. **Time**: Compounding works best over time. The longer your money stays invested, the more significant the exponential growth. Kids have a massive advantage here – they can start early and allow their investments to grow over decades.

3. **Reinvestment (turnover of capital)**: Compounding works its magic when the returns generated from investments are reinvested. This leads to the "interest-on-interest" effect, where your returns start earning returns themselves.

4. **Consistency/Discipline**: Regular contributions—no matter how small—are vital. Consistently setting aside money for savings or investment compounds your wealth over time.

## Dimensions of Compounding: Time and Rate of Return

When it comes to compounding, **time** and **rate of return** are the key dimensions. Let's break this down:

- **Time**: For young investors, time is their greatest ally. The earlier they start, the more they benefit from compounding. For instance, a child who starts saving ₹ 500 per month at the age of 15 could accumulate far more wealth by retirement than someone who starts at 30, even if the latter saves twice as much per month. This is due to the exponential growth that happens over time.

- **Rate of Return**: For older investors who may not have as much time, focusing on a higher rate of return becomes more important. However, higher returns often come with higher risks, and the balance between risk and reward must be carefully managed.

## Example 1: Time - Warren Buffett's Secret to Wealth

Warren Buffett is the perfect example of how **time** magnifies the power of compounding. Buffett started investing as a young boy and allowed his investments to grow uninterrupted for decades. By the time he turned 50, his wealth was substantial, but nearly **99% of his fortune** was built after the age of 50, thanks to the exponential growth of his investments.

Buffett's strategy was simple: invest in high-quality companies and let compounding do the work. He didn't need to generate high returns quickly – he gave his wealth the **time to compound**. The longer you stay invested, the greater the compounding effect, even with modest annual returns.

Warren Buffett, one of the wealthiest investors in the world, is a prime example of how starting early pays off. Buffett bought his first stock at the age of **11** and has been investing ever since. His philosophy has always been to invest in strong, stable companies with the potential for long-term growth. His wealth, which is now worth billions of dollars, didn't come from taking unnecessary risks but rather from **patience, time**, and the power of compounding.

Buffett has famously said, *"The stock market is designed to transfer money from the Active to the Patient."* He was able to multiply his wealth because he had decades of time on his side. As of 2024, Buffett is 93 years old, meaning he's been benefiting from compounding for over 80 years. His case shows that starting early and staying consistent is more powerful than trying to get quick gains through risky ventures.

## Warren Buffett's Wealth Growth Timeline

| Year | Age | Milestone | Wealth (Approx. USD) | Wealth (Approx. INR) | Key Details |
|---|---|---|---|---|---|
| 1930 | 0 | Born in Omaha, Nebraska, USA | N/A | N/A | Born to Howard Buffett, a stockbroker-turned congressman. |
| 1941 | 11 | Bought his first stock (3 shares of Cities Service at $38). | N/A | N/A | Began investing at a very young age. |
| 1947 | 17 | Enrolled at the University of Pennsylvania's Wharton School | N/A | N/A | Later transferred to the University of Nebraska. |

| Year | Age | Milestone | Wealth (Approx. USD) | Wealth (Approx. INR) | Key Details |
|---|---|---|---|---|---|
| 1950 | 20 | Attended Columbia Business School under Benjamin Graham. | N/A | N/A | Developed his foundational investment philosophy. |
| 1956 | 26 | Founded Buffett Partnership Ltd. | $140,000 | ₹11.62 Crore | The partnership yielded significant returns. |
| 1962 | 32 | Acquired a controlling interest in Berkshire Hathaway | $1 million+ | ₹8.3 Crore+ | Started using Berkshire as an investment vehicle. |
| 1965 | 35 | Took full control of Berkshire Hathaway | $10 million+ | ₹83 Crore+ | Began transforming it into a holding company. |
| 1970 | 40 | Became Chairman and CEO of Berkshire Hathaway | $25 million+ | ₹207.5 Crore+ | Continued growing the company. |
| 1983 | 53 | Berkshire stock reached $1,000 per share. | $620 million | ₹5,146 Crore | Buffett's net worth soared. |

| Year | Age | Milestone | Wealth (Approx. USD) | Wealth (Approx. INR) | Key Details |
|---|---|---|---|---|---|
| 1986 | 56 | Become a billionaire | $1 billion | ₹8,300 Crore | Crossed the billionaire threshold. |
| 1990s | 60–69 | Berkshire Hathaway's stock continued to rise. | $10 billion+ | ₹83,000 Crore+ | Made iconic long-term investments in consumer brands. |
| 2006 | 76 | He announced that he would donate 85% of his wealth to charity. | $40 billion+ | ₹3,32,000 Crore+ | Started his philanthropic legacy. |
| 2008 | 78 | Briefly became the richest person in the world. | $62 billion | ₹5,14,600 Crore | The global financial crisis affected his wealth. |
| 2010 | 80 | Launched the Giving Pledge with Bill Gates | $47 billion | ₹3,90,100 Crore | Philanthropy became a major focus. |
| 2020 | 90 | Berkshire Hathaway's stock continued to soar despite the pandemic. | $80 billion | ₹6,64,000 Crore | Maintained strong returns over decades. |
| 2022 | 92 | Still active as the Chairman and CEO of Berkshire Hathaway. | $100+ billion | ₹8,30,000+ Crore | Consistently among the wealthiest individuals. |

Note: INR values are approximate and based on a conversion rate of 1 USD = 83 INR. Historical exchange rates and inflation are not accounted for in these calculations.

## Example 2: Rate of Return - Rakesh Jhunjhunwala's Fast Path to Wealth

Another inspiring example is **Rakesh Jhunjhunwala,** often called the "Warren Buffett of India." Although Jhunjhunwala did not start investing as early as Buffett, he made up for it by understanding market trends and compounding his wealth through strategic investments. Starting with a small capital in the 1980s, Jhunjhunwala gradually built a portfolio that included some of India's most promising companies, such as Titan.

Jhunjhunwala's story emphasises that even if you don't have the luxury of decades, compounding can work if you combine it with the right strategies and a disciplined approach. For example, by focusing on high-growth companies and reinvesting his profits, Jhunjhunwala was able to grow his wealth significantly in a shorter time.

Rakesh Jhunjhunwala, on the other hand, didn't have as much time as Buffett, but he managed to achieve similar levels of wealth by focusing on **increasing his rate of return.** Jhunjhunwala used his capital aggressively, turning it over multiple times in a year, reinvesting profits from one trade into the next opportunity.

By **increasing the turnover of capital,** he was able to **generate higher returns in shorter time periods,** accelerating his wealth growth. While Buffett used time as his ally, Jhunjhunwala used **higher returns** and **faster reinvestment** to reach the same level of success.

# Rakesh Jhunjhunwala's Wealth Growth Timeline

| Year | Age | Milestone | Wealth (Approx.) | Key Details |
|---|---|---|---|---|
| **1960** | 0 | Born in **Mumbai, India.** | N/A | Born to an income tax officer. |
| **1985** | 25 | Started investing with **₹5,000** | ₹5,000 | Entered the stock market with initial capital. |
| **1986** | 26 | First major success with **Tata Tea** (stock price grew from ₹43 to ₹143 per share) | ₹1,00,000+ | Gained his first major profit. |
| **1990s** | 30–39 | Invested in **Titan**, which became a cornerstone of his portfolio. | ₹10 crore+ | Titan became a major contributor to his wealth. |
| **2003** | 43 | Titan's significant growth | ₹500 crore | Continued strong growth in Titan and other stocks. |
| **2008** | 48 | Survived the **global financial crisis.** | ₹5,000 crore | Retained major investments during the market downturn. |
| **2015** | 55 | Portfolio crossed ₹10,000 crore | ₹10,000 crore | Forbes ranks him as the 54th richest person in India. |

| Year | Age | Milestone | Wealth (Approx.) | Key Details |
|---|---|---|---|---|
| **2020** | 60 | Investments in **Star Health** and **Akasa Air**. | ₹30,000 crore+ | Invested in aviation and healthcare. |
| **2021** | 61 | Wealth reached ₹40,000 crore. | ₹40,000 crore | Continued strong performance in Titan and Star Health. |
| **2022** | 62 | **Passed away** on 14th August 2022 | ₹43,000 crore | Left a legacy as one of India's greatest investors. |

## Understanding the "Time Value of Money"

The "time value of money" is a key principle that ties directly into compounding. Essentially, this concept means that money today is worth more than the same amount of money in the future, due to its potential to earn interest or returns. By investing money today, it has the potential to grow, making it worth more than if you simply held onto it.

For instance, if you invest ₹ 10,000 today at an annual return of 8%, in 10 years, that amount would grow to ₹ 21,589. This is the power of compounding in action. Now imagine if you started investing regularly from a young age – the growth would be exponential.

## Why Time Favours Young Investors

One of the biggest advantages young people have is time. Let's compare two scenarios:

- **Scenario 1**: Rahul starts investing ₹500 per month at the age of 15. By the time he's 60, assuming an average return of 8% per year, he would have accumulated ₹25.30 lakh.

- **Scenario 2**: Priya starts investing ₹1,000 per month at the age of 30. By the time she's 60, assuming the same 8% return, she would accumulate ₹14,90,550/-.

Despite investing less per month, Rahul ends up with more wealth because he started 15 years earlier. This highlights how even small amounts can grow significantly when invested early.

## The Snowball Effect of Compounding

Compounding is often compared to a snowball rolling down a hill. It starts small, but as it continues rolling, it gathers more snow and grows larger. The same happens with investments. As you consistently invest and reinvest your earnings, the wealth grows exponentially.

Let's look at a **compound interest formula** to understand this mathematically:

$A = P(1+r/n)^{nt}$

Where:

- A is the final amount
- P is the principal (initial investment)
- r is the annual interest rate
- n is the number of times interest is compounded per year
- t is the time the money is invested or borrowed for

To break down the **compounding formula** into two parts—**time** and **rate of return**—and use **Warren Buffett** and **Rakesh Jhunjhunwala**.

## Breakdown into Two Parts

1. Time: The Power of Long-Term Investing (Warren Buffett Example)

The first and most important dimension of compounding is time. Warren Buffett is the perfect example of how compounding works powerfully when given enough time. Buffett started investing at a very young age and allowed his investments to compound for decades.

- The Power of Time: Compounding grows exponentially with time. Even modest returns can accumulate massive wealth over long periods. This is what Buffett leveraged. Starting in his teens and continuing into his 90s, 99% of Warren Buffett's wealth was generated after the age of 50, illustrating how compounding works slower initially but explodes later.

**Warren Buffett's Example:**

- Initial Investment: Warren started with small investments and let them grow for decades.

- Long-term Compounding: His strategy was to invest in high-quality companies and allow compounding to do its work. Over time, even small returns accumulated to billions of Dollars.

  Wealth = Initial Investment $\times (1 + r/n)^{nt}$

  Where: r is the annual interest rate

- n is the number of times interest is compounded per year

- t is the time the money is invested or borrowed for

  **Key takeaway:** Warren Buffett's success shows that the more time you give your money to compound, the larger the results will be, even with modest annual returns.

2. Rate of Return: The Power of Capital Turnover (Rakesh Jhunjhunwala Example)

The second part of the formula is the rate of return. If you don't have as much time to invest, focusing on increasing the rate of return can help you accelerate wealth-building. Here's where Rakesh Jhunjhunwala comes in. Jhunjhunwala achieved extraordinary wealth growth by increasing his capital turnover and generating higher returns in shorter periods.

- Rate of Return Breakdown:

- Rate of Interest: The return earned on your investment.

- Capital Turnover: The number of times you reinvest your capital in a year.

The more times you reinvest your profits during the year, the faster your capital grows. Jhunjhunwala didn't have as long a compounding period as Buffett, but he compensated by using a higher capital turnover to achieve rapid growth.

Wealth = Initial Investment x (1 + Rate of Interest / Capital x Turnover)^ Turnover x t

Rakesh Jhunjhunwala's Example:

- Jhunjhunwala frequently rotated his capital, reinvesting profits from one trade into another, generating higher returns in a shorter time.

- His focus was on identifying high-potential companies, investing aggressively, and turning over capital quickly to reinvest profits, leading to accelerated wealth growth.

**Key takeaway**: Jhunjhunwala's strategy shows that when time is limited, increasing the rate of return—through higher turnover and reinvesting profits quickly—can lead to fast wealth accumulation.

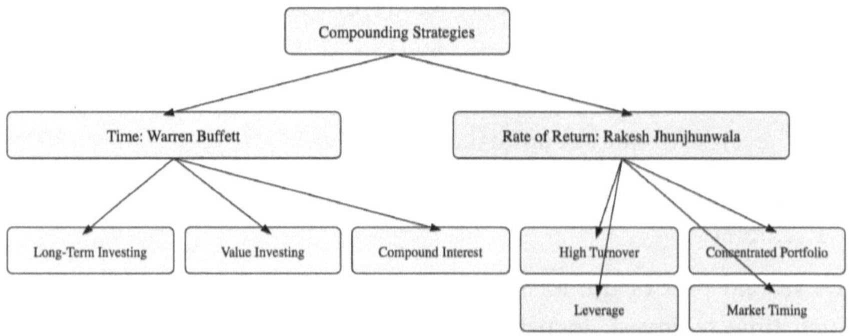


## Why the Magic of Compounding is Important for Kids

Teaching kids about the power of compounding early on is one of the greatest gifts parents can give. By helping them understand that even small savings, if consistently reinvested, can grow into substantial amounts, children can develop a long-term perspective on money. **The magic of compounding teaches kids** the importance of patience, discipline, and consistency – principles that will serve them well throughout their lives.

## Actionable Items for Parents and Teachers

1. **Start Early**: Encourage children to begin saving and investing as early as possible. Even small amounts can grow into substantial wealth over time due to the power of compounding.

2. **Use Real-Life Examples**: Share stories of Warren Buffett and Rakesh Jhunjhunwala to illustrate how compounding has worked for successful investors. This helps make the concept relatable and aspirational.

3. **Visualise Growth**: Use visual aids like graphs to show children how small investments grow exponentially over time. For example, create a savings chart that demonstrates how ₹ 500 saved each month can grow into lakhs of rupees over decades.

4. **Teach the Value of Reinvestment**: Explain the importance of reinvesting returns, whether it's interest from a savings account or dividends from an investment. The key to compounding is to reinvest rather than spend the returns.

5. **Create a Savings Plan**: Help children set up a simple savings or investment plan. Whether it's a recurring deposit or a simple ETFs investment, the idea is to get them into the habit of regularly setting aside money.

## Key Takeaways from the Chapter

1. **Start Early**: The earlier you start, the more powerful the effects of compounding will be. Time is the most critical factor in wealth-building.

2. **Small Consistent Contributions**: Even small, regular investments grow exponentially over time when combined with the power of compounding. Regular investments are the fuel that drives compounding. Small, steady contributions over time are more powerful than large, sporadic investments.

3. **The Power of Reinvestment**: Reinvesting your returns accelerates the growth of your wealth. The more you reinvest, the faster your

money grows. Don't withdraw your returns – reinvest them to keep the compounding snowball rolling.

4. **Patience is Key**: Compounding requires patience. The magic happens over the long-term, so it's crucial to stay consistent and avoid withdrawing your investments early.

5. **Teach Compounding Early**: Introducing the concept of compounding to children will set them up for long-term financial success. Parents and teachers should encourage saving and investing habits early on.

## Call to Action: Commit to Long-Term Growth

Make the commitment today to start investing consistently. Whether it's ₹500 or ₹5,000, the amount doesn't matter as much as staying regular. Set up an automatic investment plan that pulls a fixed amount of money from your account every month, ensuring that you don't miss out on the power of compounding.

Reflect on your financial goals and think about how you can maximise the time factor in your investments. Every year you delay starting will cost you thousands (or even lakhs) in lost growth potential. The sooner you begin, the more powerful compounding will be for you.

## Reflection: Your Compounding Journey

Take a moment to think about your current saving and investing habits. Are you consistent with your investments? Could you be doing more to harness the power of compounding?

- What are you currently doing to let your money grow over time?

- Are there areas where you can improve your consistency?

- How much time do you have left to let compounding work its magic?

Write down your thoughts and consider what steps you can take today to ensure a stronger financial future.

## Summary: The Magic of Compounding

"One of the most powerful lessons from the wealth timelines of great investors like Warren Buffett and Rakesh Jhunjhunwala is that **two-thirds of their wealth was built in the last one-third of their lives**. This is the power of compounding – patience and consistency over decades lead to exponential wealth growth. Compounding starts slow but accelerates significantly as your investments grow larger. The key takeaway: **Start early, stay consistent, and give your wealth time to grow.**"

Compounding is not a one-time event but a continuous process that relies on consistency, patience, and time. The most critical part of your journey is staying committed to your regular investments and giving them the time they need to grow.

The third "C"—**Compounding**—completes the **Wealth Infinity Cycle**, building on the foundations of **commitment** and **consistency**. By starting early, investing regularly, and letting your returns grow exponentially, you'll position yourself for long-term financial success.

## Conclusion

Compounding is the foundation of long-term wealth-building. By understanding the components of compounding and how it works over time, children can develop the habits and mindset necessary to grow their wealth in the future. With time on their side, young investors have a unique advantage and can set themselves up for lifelong financial success by starting early, reinvesting returns, and being patient.

# Part 2

# Mastering Market Investment Fundamentals

. . . . . . . . . . . . . . . . . . . . . . . . . . . . . . . . . . . . . . . . . . .

"Investing wisely is not about luck; it's about
understanding the fundamentals, managing risks,
and letting growth unfold over time."

— Talanki Naveen Kumar Guptha

. . . . . . . . . . . . . . . . . . . . . . . . . . . . . . . . . . . . . . . . . . .

# Chapter 7

# The First Step into the Stock Market – Starting with Index ETFs

Entering the stock market can seem intimidating, especially for younger investors or beginners. However, one of the best ways to get started is with **Index ETFs (Exchange-Traded Funds)**. These offer a low-risk, diversified entry into investing, making them ideal for kids and teens who are learning about the stock market for the first time.

In this chapter, we will explain why Index ETFs are a smart choice for beginners, guide you through the process of opening a trading (brokerage) account, and provide actionable steps for buying your first ETFs. With the power of commitment, consistency, and compounding behind you, your wealth-building journey begins here.

## What Are Index ETFs?

An **Index ETFs** is a type of investment fund that tracks a specific index, such as the **Nifty 50** or the **S&P 500**. When you buy an Index ETFs, you're essentially buying a small piece of every company in that index. This provides instant diversification, which reduces your risk compared to buying individual stocks.

For example, if you invest in an **NSE Nifty 50 ETFs**, you are investing in 50 of the largest companies listed on the National Stock Exchange of India. Instead of betting on the success of just one company, your investment is spread across several companies, which reduces the likelihood of severe losses.

## Why Index ETFs Are a Great Starting Point

1. **Diversification**: By investing in an ETFs, you own a small share of multiple companies, spreading out the risk.

2. **Lower Risk**: ETFs generally carry lower risk compared to individual stocks because they follow an index's performance rather than relying on one company's success.

3. **Simplicity**: ETFs are easy to buy and sell, much like individual stocks, and they usually have lower fees compared to actively managed funds.

4. **Passive Investing**: Unlike actively managing a portfolio, ETFs require minimal maintenance. You don't need to pick and choose stocks yourself – the index does the work for you.

## Diagram: How an Index ETFs Works

### How an Index ETF Works

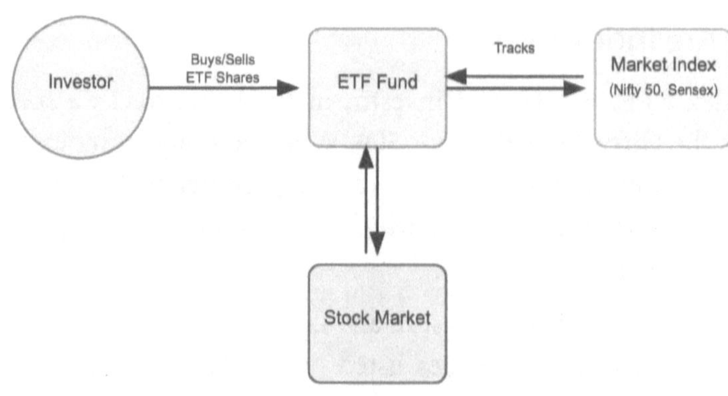


This diagram will show the basic structure of an Index ETFs:

- Investor buys an ETFs.

- ETFs tracks a broad index (e.g., Nifty 50, Bank Nifty, etc.).

- ETFs automatically adjusts to reflect changes in the index (companies being added or removed).

- The value of the ETFs fluctuates based on the performance of the overall index.

## Step-by-Step Guide to Opening a Trading (Brokerage) Account

Before you can invest in an ETFs, you need to open a brokerage account. Here's a simple guide to get you started:

**Step 1: Choose a Brokerage Platform**

Many online platforms in India make it easy to open a brokerage account, such as **Zerodha**, **Upstox**, and **Groww**. Look for a platform that offers:

- Low or zero brokerage fees.

- User-friendly interface.

- Access to a wide range of ETFs.

**Step 2: Complete KYC**

The next step is to complete the **KYC (Know Your Customer)** process. You'll need to provide identification documents such as:

- PAN card.

- Aadhaar card or passport.

- A photo and your signature.

This process usually takes just a few days, and many platforms allow you to complete it online.

**Step 3: Fund Your Account**

Once your account is set up, you'll need to transfer funds from your bank account into your trading (brokerage) account. You can decide how much to transfer based on your budget for your first ETFs purchase.

**Step 4: Search for an Index ETFs**

After funding your account, it's time to search for an **Index ETFs**. Look for ones that track broad indices like:

- **Nifty 50 ETFs**: Tracks the top 50 companies listed on the National Stock Exchange.
- **Bank Nifty ETFs**: Tracks the largest banks listed on the National Stock Exchange.
- **Nifty Next 50 ETFs**

**Step 5: Place Your First Order**

Once you've chosen an ETFs, place your buy order. Most platforms allow you to input the quantity or amount you want to invest. After confirming the order, the ETFs will be added to your portfolio.

Congratulations! You're officially a stock market investor.

## Example: Aryan's First Investment

Aryan, an 18-year-old eager to start his wealth-building journey, followed these steps to buy his first ETFs. After saving ₹5,000 from his pocket money and birthday gifts, he opened an account on **Zerodha**, completed the KYC process, and transferred his money.

He chose the **Nifty 50 ETFs** because it offered him exposure to 50 top Indian companies. Over the next few years, Aryan consistently added small amounts to his portfolio. By sticking to the principles of commitment and consistency, his portfolio grew steadily, benefiting from both market growth and the power of compounding.

## Low-Risk Investment for Kids

While ETFs are generally safer than individual stocks, it's still essential to understand that no investment is entirely risk-free. However, Index ETFs offer a level of protection through diversification. As a young investor, this reduces the likelihood of losing large amounts of money early on, which can be discouraging.

## Key Advantages of ETFs for Kids and Beginners

- **Affordability**: Many ETFs have a low minimum investment requirement, making them accessible even with limited funds.

- **Automatic Diversification**: Rather than worrying about picking the "right" stock, investing in an ETFs automatically diversifies your investment.

- **Long-Term Growth Potential**: Index ETFs provide exposure to top-performing companies that tend to grow in value over time.

## Quote to Reflect On

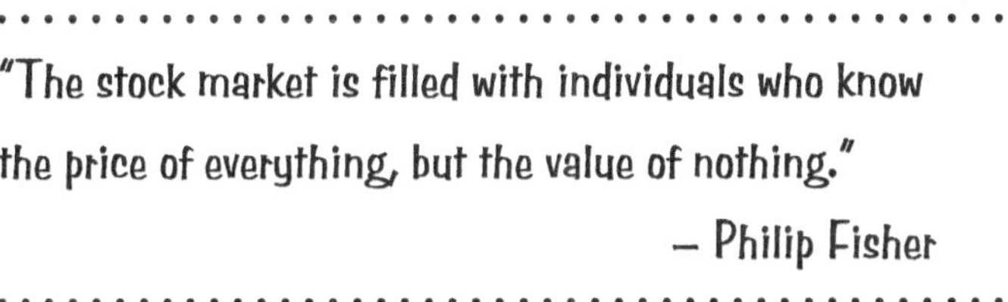


This quote reminds young investors that stepping into the stock market can feel uncomfortable at first, but the potential rewards make it worth the effort.

## Key Takeaways

1. **Start Small, Think Big**: You don't need a lot of money to begin investing. ETFs offer a way to start small while still gaining exposure to a broad market.

2. **Diversification is Key**: Investing in an Index ETFs spreads your money across many companies, lowering your risk.

3. **Focus on Consistency**: Even if you can only invest a small amount each month, staying consistent will lead to compounding benefits over time.

## Call to Action: Take Your First Step into Investing

Ready to get started? Follow these steps to open your first trading (brokerage) account, fund it, and purchase your first ETFs. The sooner you begin, the more time your money will have to grow. Don't wait for the "perfect" moment to start – investing is about time in the market, not timing the market.

## Reflection: Your First ETFs Purchase

- Have you opened a trading (brokerage) account yet? If not, what's holding you back?

- What amount can you realistically set aside to make your first ETFs investment?

- Are you ready to commit to a regular investment schedule, even if it's a small amount each month?

Reflect on these questions as you prepare to take the first step in your investing journey.

## Summary: Starting Small with Low-Risk Investments

In this chapter, we explored how Index ETFs provide an excellent low-risk option for beginners to start investing. These funds offer diversification, affordability, and simplicity – everything a young investor needs to dip their toes into the stock market without overwhelming risks. By following the simple steps outlined here, you can open a brokerage account, choose an ETFs, and begin your wealth-building journey.

This is your first tangible step towards implementing the **Wealth Infinity Cycle**. With commitment and consistency, your investments will start to grow, and you will benefit from the power of **compounding**.

## Conclusion

Investing doesn't have to be complicated or risky, especially when you start with **Index ETFs**. These low-risk, diversified investments allow you to gain exposure to the stock market without the pressure of picking individual stocks. As you continue on your journey, the lessons of commitment, consistency, and compounding will remain at the core of your wealth-building strategy.

In the next chapter, we will delve deeper into the importance of risk management and how it can protect you from potential pitfalls in the stock market. Understanding risk is critical to becoming a successful investor, so stay tuned for more actionable insights and strategies.

# Chapter 8

# The Importance of Risk Management in Investing

Investing is a powerful tool for building wealth, but it is not without risk. Risk management is crucial in protecting your hard-earned money from market fluctuations and making sure you don't lose more than you're willing to. It's essential to understand that risk and reward go hand in hand – higher returns often come with greater risks.

In this chapter, we will explore the importance of risk management in investing, teach you basic strategies to minimise risk, and use practical examples, a case study, and a diagram to solidify these concepts. As you build your investment portfolio, knowing how to manage risk is just as important as choosing where to invest.

## What is Risk in Investing?

In the context of investing, **risk** refers to the possibility of losing money or not achieving the expected returns. Stock prices can fluctuate due to changes in the economy, industry conditions, company performance, or even global events. While no investment is entirely risk-free, understanding and managing risk can help you minimise potential losses.

There are various types of risks in investing:

1. **Market Risk**: The risk that the overall stock market will decline, affecting all investments.

2. **Company-Specific Risk**: The risk associated with a specific company, such as poor performance or scandals.

3. **Liquidity Risk**: The risk of not being able to sell an investment when needed due to a lack of buyers.

4. **Inflation Risk**: The risk that inflation will erode the value of your returns over time.

## Diagram: Types of Investment Risks

A diagram here will visualise the different types of risks mentioned above (Market, Company-Specific, Liquidity, Inflation), showing how they affect your investments and what they mean for a portfolio.

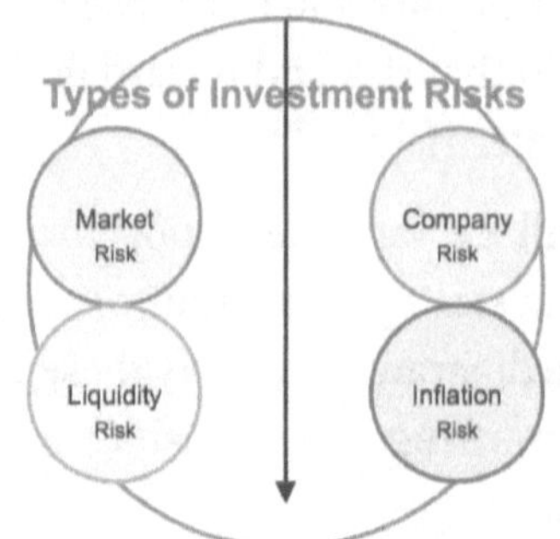


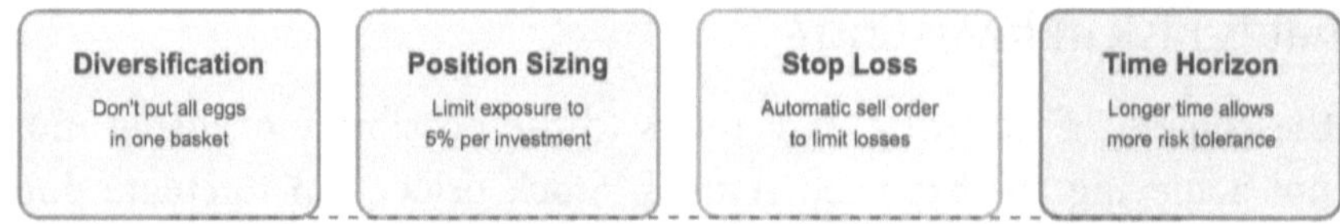


*Integrated Risk Management Strategy*

## The Core Principles of Risk Management

### 1. Diversification

**Diversification** is one of the most fundamental strategies for managing risk. The idea is simple: don't put all your eggs in one basket. By spreading your investments across different assets (stocks, bonds, ETFs, etc.), industries, or even geographic locations, you reduce the chance that a single bad investment will significantly hurt your portfolio.

For example, if you invest only in tech companies and the tech sector crashes, your entire portfolio will suffer. However, if you diversify by investing in technology, healthcare, and real estate, a loss in one sector may be offset by gains in another.

## 2. Position Sizing (Allocation)

Another key principle in risk management is **position sizing**, which refers to the amount of money you allocate to a single investment. Instead of putting a large portion of your capital into one stock or ETFs, consider limiting your exposure to a small percentage of your total portfolio.

A good rule of thumb is to invest no more than 5% of your portfolio in any single stock. For young investors starting out, this might mean limiting your initial investments to small amounts and gradually increasing as you gain confidence.

## 3. Setting Stop Losses

A **stop-loss** is an automatic order placed with your broker to sell a stock if it drops to a certain price. This prevents you from holding on to a losing position for too long. Stop losses can help protect your portfolio from large losses in case the market turns against you.

For instance, if you buy a stock for ₹500 and set a stop-loss at ₹450, your stock will be sold automatically if its price drops to ₹450, limiting your loss to 10%. This way, you avoid emotional decision-making and lock in some protection against further declines.

## 4. Understanding Time Horizon

Your **time horizon** refers to how long you plan to hold your investments. Typically, the longer your time horizon, the more risk you can afford to take. This is because short-term fluctuations in the market are less likely to impact you if you're investing for the long run.

For young investors, a long time horizon can allow you to ride out market downturns and benefit from the power of compounding over time.

### Example: Risk in Real-Life

Let's take the example of Rohan and Ishaan, two young investors. Rohan decided to invest all his savings in one hot stock – let's say a popular tech startup. For a while, the stock did well, but when the company faced unexpected challenges, its stock price plummeted. Since Rohan hadn't diversified, he lost a large portion of his money.

Ishaan, on the other hand, spread his investments across an ETFs tracking the **Nifty 50**, some bonds, and a few individual stocks in different industries. Even though the same tech stock in his portfolio fell, his losses were much smaller because his other investments remained stable or even grew in value.

Rohan took on **too much risk**, while Ishaan practised **diversification** – a key principle of risk management.

## Case Study: The Fall of Kingfisher Airlines

Let's dive into a real-life example that highlights the importance of risk management. Kingfisher Airlines was once one of India's most popular airlines, founded by Vijay Mallya. It had a strong brand and a significant market share, attracting many investors. However, Kingfisher began experiencing financial trouble due to rising fuel costs, poor management, and heavy debt.

Many investors who had put a large portion of their portfolios into Kingfisher lost nearly all their money when the company went bankrupt in 2012. Had these investors diversified across different industries, they would have been better insulated from such a catastrophic loss. The lesson here? Even companies that seem like safe bets can fail, and that's why risk management is essential.

## Quote to Reflect On

. . . . . . . . . . . . . . . . . . . . . . . . . . . . . . . . . . . . . . . . .

"The essence of investment management

is the management of risks,

not the management of returns."

– Benjamin Graham

. . . . . . . . . . . . . . . . . . . . . . . . . . . . . . . . . . . . . . . . .

This quote by Benjamin Graham, a legendary investor and mentor to Warren Buffett, reminds us that managing risk is more important than chasing high returns. Without a proper risk management strategy, you might win big occasionally, but you could also lose it all.

## Key Takeaways

1. **Diversification is essential**: By spreading your investments across different assets, you reduce the impact of a single bad investment.

2. **Position sizing limits risk**: Never put too much of your portfolio into one stock or asset.

3. **Stop losses protect your capital**: Setting automatic stop losses ensures that you don't hold onto a losing position for too long.

4. **Understand your time horizon**: The longer your investment timeline, the more risk you can afford to take.

## Call to Action: Review Your Current Risk Management Plan

- Do you have a diversified portfolio, or are you overly reliant on one type of investment?

- Are you using stop losses to protect yourself from steep declines in the market?

- How much of your portfolio is invested in any single stock or sector? Is it more than 5%?

Take a moment to review your current investments and make adjustments if needed to better manage your risk.

## Reflections: How Do You Feel About Risk?

- Have you ever experienced significant losses in the stock market? What could you have done differently to mitigate the risk?

- How comfortable are you with risk? Are you more inclined to take risks for higher returns, or do you prefer more conservative investments?

Understanding your risk tolerance will help you create a better investment strategy moving forward.

## Summary: Protecting Your Portfolio Through Risk Management

Risk is an inevitable part of investing, but it doesn't have to be scary. With proper risk management techniques like diversification, position sizing, and setting stop losses, you can minimise the chances of losing significant portions of your portfolio. By understanding your time horizon and risk tolerance, you'll be better equipped to navigate the ups and downs of the stock market.

In our next chapter, we'll delve into a transformative concept I call the **Wealth Infinity Cycle**. This powerful framework demonstrates how methodical investing paired with intelligent risk management creates an unstoppable momentum toward lasting wealth. Think of risk management as more than just a defensive shield – it's the foundation that enables sustained success and exponential growth over time. When mastered, this cycle becomes a self-reinforcing engine of wealth creation.

## Conclusion

The path to wealth creation requires taking risks, but those risks should be calculated and managed wisely. As you continue your journey, always remember that risk management is the cornerstone of successful investing. It will protect you during downturns and ensure that your capital is preserved for future growth.

# Chapter 9

# The Wealth Infinity Cycle in Action: Compounding Growth Through Vision and Habit

## Compounding Beyond Investing

When we think of "compounding," the mind typically goes to financial growth through investments. But what if I told you that compounding is far more powerful than just growing money? Compounding is an exponential growth principle that applies to any area where consistent effort, strategic reinvestment, and habit-building are practised. This chapter will show how the Wealth Infinity Cycle—the loop of commitment, consistency, and compounding—drives progress, not just in finance, but in any pursuit we commit ourselves to.

Imagine starting a new project or developing a new skill. At first, it might seem like a small effort that yields little return. However, when done repeatedly, with intentional reinvestment into improving, these efforts grow beyond what you initially expected. By repeating this cycle, we can build something far greater than the sum of each action – compounding growth is at work.

## Commitment to a Larger Vision

Every journey begins with a clear goal. Commitment is our dedication to that goal, even when obstacles arise. The Wealth Infinity Cycle begins with a vision and the resolve to pursue it. This commitment pushes us to move forward, whether it's in creating a new product, building a business, or developing a life-changing skill. It requires saying "yes" to your goal daily and seeing it through, even when progress feels slow.

For example, Elon Musk, the visionary entrepreneur, committed himself to the goals of sustainable energy and space exploration. He knew these pursuits would be challenging, but his commitment was rooted in something deeper than personal success. His vision, once just an idea, led him to develop technologies like reusable rockets and electric cars. His commitment to a future he believed in allowed him to persevere through immense challenges. Every action toward that vision compounded over time, creates world-changing advancements.

## Consistency: Research, Development and Skill Acquisition

After setting a goal, the next essential part of the cycle is consistency. Compounding happens because of regular, repeated effort. Just like a single investment grows as we add to it over time, a skill or project grows through consistent improvement. This includes regular research, practice, and development – all of which lead to mastery and innovation.

Take J.K. Rowling, for instance. Before she became the globally celebrated author of *Harry Potter*, she spent years honing her craft. Despite early rejections, Rowling kept writing, refining her story and characters, and persevering with the belief that her work would eventually connect with readers. Her consistency turned each page into part of a literary world that captivated millions. This compounding of effort over time built not just a book but an entire franchise.

When we remain consistent in research and development, we are effectively reinvesting our energy and time. Each effort compounds, pushing us closer to our goal.

## Monetising and Reinvesting for Exponential Growth

The next stage of the Wealth Infinity Cycle is monetising and reinvesting our efforts. In financial investing, compounding happens when we reinvest earnings. Similarly, in personal or professional projects, compounding occurs when we reinvest time, skills, and proceeds back into our goals. This reinvestment doesn't just maintain our growth – it accelerates it.

Returning to Elon Musk, once Tesla and SpaceX started generating revenue, he didn't stop at "good enough." He reinvested profits into further R&D, creating innovations that fuelled even more growth. This approach allowed him to advance faster than competitors and continually break new ground. His reinvestment compounded the impact of each venture, amplifying his initial vision into world-changing technologies.

When we monetise our skills or ideas, whether financially or through other forms of value, it enables us to reinvest that outcome. This cycle of reinvestment pushes us into a new level of growth, allowing us to see returns that wouldn't be possible without that reinvestment.

## Repeating the Cycle: The Path to Exponential Success

The power of the Wealth Infinity Cycle lies in its ability to repeat indefinitely. Each cycle builds upon the last, compounding growth further each time. The first step is often the hardest, but once momentum is achieved, each repetition creates more and more growth. The Wealth Infinity Cycle functions like a flywheel: slow to start, but once it's moving, it keeps going with less and less effort.

For example, J.K. Rowling's success didn't stop with the publication of her first book. Each subsequent book reinvested her time, skill, and brand value into expanding the *Harry Potter* universe. Rowling went on to create spin-offs, merchandise, and new stories that connected with an ever-growing fan base. Her initial commitment to writing compounded into a phenomenon that spans multiple generations, all because she kept cycling through commitment, consistency, and reinvestment.

The same approach can apply in any area of life, from personal growth to entrepreneurship. When we understand and apply the Wealth Infinity Cycle, we create an engine of continuous, compounding growth, leading us to achieve goals we once thought impossible.

## Key Takeaways

1. **Compounding Goes Beyond Finance**: Compounding is a principle that can be applied anywhere we put consistent effort and reinvest in improvement.

2. **Commitment to a Clear Vision is Foundational**: A clear vision and commitment allow us to endure challenges and pursue long-term goals.

3. **Consistency Compounds Value Over Time**: Regular, repeated efforts lay the foundation for exponential growth.

4. **Reinvestment Drives Exponential Growth**: By reinvesting time, skills, or earnings, we compound growth and progress faster.

5. **The Cycle of Repetition Fuels Lasting Success**: Each cycle builds upon the last, creating a powerful, continuous growth loop.

## Reflection Questions

- Where in your life can you apply the Wealth Infinity Cycle to grow and achieve a goal?

- What consistent actions can you start taking towards your goal?

- How can you reinvest your progress back into this area to help it grow further?

Reflecting on these questions can help you identify areas where you can harness the Wealth Infinity Cycle for growth in both personal and financial pursuits.

## Call to Action

Identify one area of your life or a project you're passionate about. Outline steps to practice commitment and consistency within this area. Think about how you can create value, whether that's financial, personal, or educational. Plan to reinvest the value or returns from this effort back into the cycle, fuelling further growth. The Wealth Infinity Cycle doesn't demand perfection, only dedication and perseverance. Start small, be consistent, and watch the power of compounding take effect.

## Conclusion

The Wealth Infinity Cycle demonstrates that the principles of investing—commitment, consistency, and compounding—can transform any pursuit, not just financial investments. Whether you're an entrepreneur, writer, artist, or professional, these principles create pathways for significant growth and personal development. Compounding applies to all areas of life, and by repeating the cycle, you can build something greater than each action alone.

## Summary

In this chapter, we explored how the Wealth Infinity Cycle applies beyond finance, showing how disciplined actions can compound over time to create monumental achievements. We looked at inspiring examples, from Elon Musk's ventures to J.K. Rowling's creative journey, which illustrate the profound impact of commitment, consistency, and reinvestment.

Now that we understand the Wealth Infinity Cycle in the context of personal growth and vision, we'll turn to building an investment portfolio. The next chapter will dive into practical steps for creating a diversified portfolio, starting small and growing big – applying the principles of the Wealth Infinity Cycle directly to financial investments.

This chapter weaves together motivation, actionable steps, and practical applications for readers, setting them up to apply the Wealth Infinity Cycle as they start building their portfolios in the following chapter.

# Chapter 10

# How to Build Your First Portfolio: Start Small, Grow Big

Building your first portfolio can be one of the most exciting steps in your wealth-building journey. This chapter will guide you through the process of selecting your first investments, balancing risk and reward, and setting up a portfolio that grows with you over time. The key is to **start small** and focus on growing steadily, using the principles of commitment, consistency, and compounding that we've discussed.

**Understanding What a Portfolio Is**

A **portfolio** is simply a collection of financial assets you own. These assets can include:

- **Stocks**: Shares in individual companies.

- **Exchange-Traded Funds (ETFs)**: Baskets of stocks or bonds that track a particular index (like the Nifty 50 in India or the S&P 500 in the US).

- **Mutual Funds**: Pooled investments managed by professionals.

- **Bonds**: Loans you make to companies or governments that pay interest over time.

A diversified portfolio contains a mix of these different types of investments to spread risk and improve the chances of achieving your financial goals.

## Start Small: The Power of Incremental Growth

One of the biggest myths about investing is that you need a lot of money to get started. In reality, you can begin with just a few hundred rupees. The important thing is to get started and contribute regularly. Even small amounts can grow significantly over time with consistency and compounding.

## Example: Starting Small with Index ETFs

Suppose you are a 16-year-old and you have ₹1,000 to invest each month. A simple way to start would be to invest in a **low-cost Index ETFs** like the **Nifty 50 ETFs**. This ETFs tracks the performance of the top 50 companies in India and provides instant diversification with a single investment.

After one year of consistent investing, you will have invested ₹12,000. Let's say the stock market grows at an average annual return of 10%. At the end of the year, your portfolio will have grown to approximately ₹13,200. While this may seem small at first, the key is to stay consistent. Over time, the power of compounding will take over.

## Quote to Reflect On

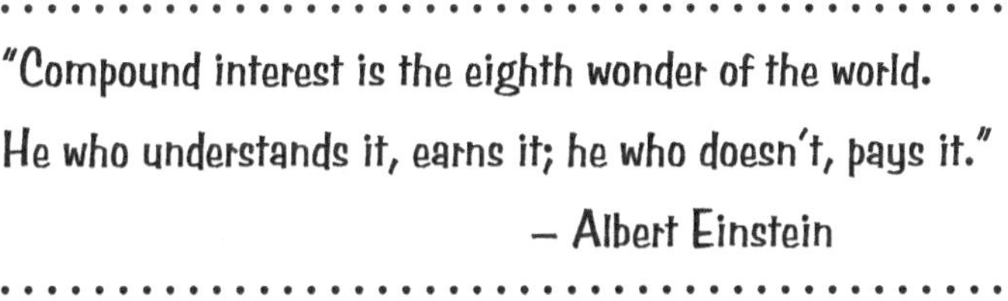


This quote highlights the importance of starting early and letting your investments compound over time. Even small contributions can lead to significant wealth if given enough time.

## Steps to Building Your First Portfolio

### Step 1: Set Your Financial Goals

Before you start investing, it's essential to define what you want to achieve. Your goals could be short-term, such as saving for college, or long-term, like building wealth for retirement. Understanding your goals will help you decide on the best investment strategy for your portfolio.

### Step 2: Choose Low-Risk Investments

For beginners, it's wise to start with low-risk options like Index ETFs or mutual funds. These options provide diversification (reducing risk) and are less volatile than investing in individual stocks.

- **Index ETFs**: As mentioned earlier, an Index ETFs tracks the performance of a market index like the Nifty 50. This gives you exposure to the entire market rather than betting on individual companies.

- **Mutual Funds**: A mutual fund is managed by professionals who invest your money in a variety of stocks or bonds. For young investors, a **balanced mutual fund** (which holds both stocks and bonds) can be a good option to start with.

**Step 3: Diversify Your Portfolio**

One of the key principles of risk management is diversification. **Diversification** means spreading your investments across different assets (stocks, bonds, ETFs, etc.) and sectors (technology, healthcare, finance, etc.) to reduce risk.

- **Example**: Instead of putting all your money in one stock (like Reliance Industries), you could invest in a mix of sectors – perhaps an ETFs that tracks the entire Indian stock market, plus some bonds to balance out the risk.

**Step 4: Keep Costs Low**

When building your first portfolio, it's important to choose low-cost investments. High fees can eat into your returns over time. **Index funds** and **ETFs** tend to have lower fees than actively managed funds, making them a good choice for young investors starting out.

**Step 5: Monitor and Adjust Your Portfolio**

As you continue to invest, regularly monitor your portfolio to ensure it aligns with your financial goals. Rebalance your investments if necessary, but avoid making impulsive decisions based on short-term market movements.

## Case Study: Divya's Journey to Building a Portfolio

Let's look at the case of **Divya**, a 17-year-old who started with ₹5,000 she had saved from her part-time job. Divya wanted to start investing but didn't know much about the stock market. After researching, she decided to put her money into a **Nifty 50 Index ETFs** because it was a low-risk way to get exposure to the stock market.

Over the next two years, Divya consistently contributed ₹1,000 every month to her ETFs. By the time she turned 19, her portfolio had grown to ₹28,000, with an average return of 12% per year. Divya didn't panic during market dips; she continued investing, confident in the long-term growth of the market.

As her income increased, Divya started diversifying her portfolio, adding some bonds and mutual funds for extra stability. By the time she graduated from college, her consistent investments and diversification had built a strong foundation for long-term wealth.

## The Role of Time in Portfolio Growth

A key component of portfolio growth is **time**. The longer you stay invested, the more your wealth can grow due to compounding returns. This is why it's important not to panic and sell when the market drops.

## Common Mistakes to Avoid

When building your first portfolio, it's important to avoid some common pitfalls:

1. **Over-concentrating in One Asset**: Putting all your money in one stock or sector increases risk. Diversification is key.

2. **Chasing High Returns**: It's tempting to invest in "hot" stocks that promise big returns, but these often come with high risk.

3. **Frequent Trading**: Constantly buying and selling can lead to higher fees and tax implications, which can erode your returns. Stick to your plan and avoid emotional reactions to market swings.

## Quote to Reflect On

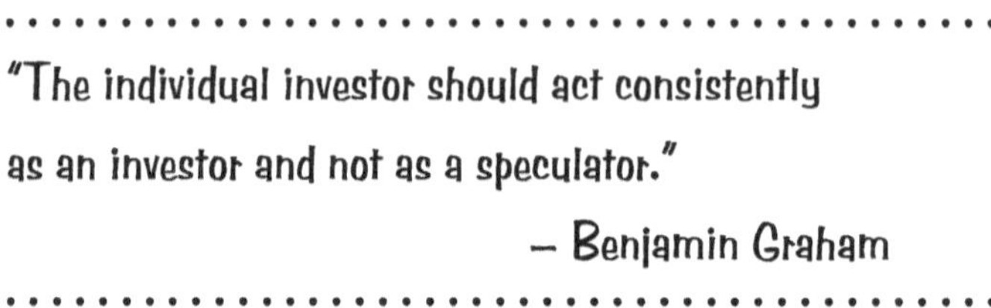


This quote reminds us to focus on the long-term growth of our investments and avoid the temptation of short-term speculation. Building a strong portfolio is about staying committed to your plan and being patient.

## Key Takeaways

1. **Start small but consistently**: Even small amounts can grow into significant wealth with time and compounding.

2. **Diversify your investments**: Spread your money across different assets to reduce risk.

3. **Choose low-cost options**: Focus on investments like Index ETFs and mutual funds that have low fees.

4. **Avoid emotional investing**: Stick to your long-term plan and avoid making decisions based on short-term market fluctuations.

**Call to Action: Build Your First Portfolio**

- Set your financial goals and decide on an investment strategy.

- Open a brokerage account if you don't have one already.

- Choose a low-cost, diversified ETFs or mutual fund to get started.

- Start small, contribute regularly, and be patient as your portfolio grows.

**Reflections: Are You Ready to Build Wealth?**

- How much can you start investing today, even if it's a small amount?

- What kind of investments would align with your financial goals?

- Are you prepared to stay committed and consistent for the long-term?

Think about the type of portfolio that best suits your needs and start building today.

## Summary: Start Small, Grow Big

Building your first portfolio is a critical step in your financial journey. By starting small, focusing on low-risk, low-cost investments, and being consistent, you can build a portfolio that grows steadily over time. The earlier you start, the more time you give your investments to compound, leading to exponential growth.

## Conclusion

Your first portfolio doesn't need to be complex. Start with what you have, make consistent contributions, and allow the power of compounding to work over time. By focusing on diversification and managing risk, you'll be on your way to building lasting wealth.

# Part 3

# Developing Financial Wisdom

# Chapter 11

# Understanding Market Trends: How to Watch the Market Without Panic

**Key Focus:** Strategic Patience in long-term investing.

Investing requires time, patience, and consistency. One of the greatest challenges for new investors, especially those starting young, is learning how to stay calm during market fluctuations. In this chapter, we focus on understanding market trends in the context of **Indian indices** like the **Nifty 50** and **Bank Nifty**, and how staying invested in **ETFs** (Exchange-Traded Funds) helps you build wealth over the long-term. The goal here is to understand that compounding works best when you resist the urge to panic during market downturns and allow your investments to grow over time.

## Introduction: Staying in the Market, Not Just Holding Stocks

Investing in India offers excellent growth opportunities, but the market can be volatile. For young investors, this can be unsettling. However, holding onto an investment strategy over the long-term—through good and bad times—often yields better returns than trying to time the market.

It's important to remember that long-term investing doesn't necessarily mean holding on to a single stock or ETFs forever. Instead, it means **staying invested in the market over the years** to benefit from the power of compounding. By using low-cost Index ETFs like those tracking the **Nifty 50** or **Bank Nifty**, young investors can stay diversified and minimise risk.

## The Nature of Market Trends: Indian Stock Market Cycles

Like all stock markets, **Indian stock markets** move in cycles. There are bull markets, where stock prices rise, and bear markets, where they fall. These cycles are part of the market's natural rhythm. For instance, in India, the **Nifty 50** index has seen many ups and downs, but the overall trend has been positive over the long-term.

- **Example**: If you look at the Nifty 50 index over the last 10 years, despite short-term market corrections (like in 2020 during the pandemic), it has grown steadily, delivering strong long-term returns.

## Why Panic Hurts Long-Term Investing

Investors who panic and sell during a downturn often lock in losses. More importantly, they miss out on the eventual recovery, which is where the magic of compounding kicks in. The **Sensex** has consistently shown growth over the decades, despite short-term market corrections.

**Example: Missing the Recovery**

Consider a young investor who started investing in a **Nifty 50 Index ETFs** in 2018. The pandemic market crash of March 2020 caused the Nifty 50 to fall significantly. If that investor had panicked and sold their ETFs units, they would have crystallised their losses. However, by holding through the downturn, they would have seen their investment recover and grow when the market rebounded by the end of 2020.

The Nifty 50 reached record highs in the following years, proving that **staying invested** is more important than trying to time the market.

## The Power of Patience in Compounding

Compounding works best over long periods. This means that the longer you remain invested, the greater your returns will be. However, compounding requires patience, and **staying in the market through all its ups and downs** is key to leveraging this principle.

## Case Study: Staying Invested in Indian Markets

Let's look at a real-life case study from India to highlight the importance of staying invested. During the **2008 financial crisis**, the Sensex fell by more than 50%. Many investors panicked and sold their holdings, locking in their losses. However, those who stayed invested saw the market recover over the next few years, with the Sensex crossing 30,000 points by 2017.

## Example: Holding Through Crises

Investors who purchased ETFs tracking the **Nifty 50** or **Bank Nifty** before the 2008 crash and held on through the downturn saw their investments recover and even double in value by the mid-2010s. This shows the importance of patience and the benefits of compounding when investing for the long-term.

## Strategies to Stay Calm During Market Fluctuations

Staying calm during market downturns is easier said than done. However, there are several strategies that can help:

1. **Understand the Long-Term Perspective**:

   Historically, the **Indian stock market** has recovered from every downturn and reached new highs. Keep this in mind when short-term volatility occurs.

2. **Diversification with ETFs**:

   By investing in a diversified basket of securities through Index ETFs (such as those tracking the Nifty 50), you minimise your risk compared to investing in individual stocks.

3. **Automated Investing**:

   Use **Systematic Investment Plans (SIPs)** to automatically invest a fixed amount in an ETFs every month. This ensures that you are investing regularly, regardless of market conditions, and reduces the emotional pressure of market timing.

4. **Avoid Checking Your Portfolio Daily**:

   Constantly monitoring your investments can increase anxiety. Instead, check your portfolio periodically—say every quarter or annually—so you don't react emotionally to every market move.

## The Negative Impact of Emotional Decisions

Emotional decision-making in investing often leads to poor results. Many investors buy during bull markets out of greed and sell during bear markets out of fear. This practice can erode long-term returns, especially for young investors.

## Case Study: The 2020 Market Crash in India

The 2020 market crash, triggered by the COVID-19 pandemic, saw the Nifty 50 drop sharply in March. Investors who panicked and sold their ETFs during this time locked in their losses. However, those who stayed patient saw the Nifty 50 recover by the end of 2020 and eventually reach record highs by 2021. This example demonstrates the risks of emotional investing and the importance of sticking to your long-term plan.

## Call to Action: Building Emotional Resilience

Here are actionable steps to help you stay focused on your long-term investing goals:

- **Set Long-Term Financial Goals**: Write down your investment goals, whether it's saving for higher education, buying a house, or retirement. When the market fluctuates, refer back to these goals to remind yourself why you're investing.

- **Use SIPs to Stay Disciplined**: A SIP (Systematic Investment Plan) is an excellent way to automate your investments and remove emotional decision-making. Whether the market is up or down, your SIP will continue to invest on a regular basis.

- **Diversify Your Investments**: Consider investing in multiple ETFs that track different indices or sectors. This can reduce risk and increase your chances of long-term success.

## Key Takeaways

1. **Compounding requires patience**: The longer you stay invested, the more your wealth grows through compounding.

2. **Avoid emotional decisions**: Panic selling during downturns locks in losses and prevents you from benefiting from market recoveries.

3. **Diversification and SIPs reduce risk**: Use SIPs to stay disciplined and diversify your investments to lower risk.

4. **Market downturns are temporary**: Historically, the **Nifty 50** and **Bank Nifty** have always recovered from corrections, rewarding those who stay invested.

## Reflections

1. Do you feel anxious when the market goes down? What steps can you take to develop more patience in your investment journey?

2. How can you ensure that you're not checking your portfolio too often and making emotional decisions?

## Conclusion

Patience is key to unlocking the power of compounding. In the Indian market, indices like the Nifty 50 and Sensex have proven that staying invested over the long-term delivers strong returns, even in the face of short-term volatility. By diversifying, automating your investments through SIPs, and keeping a calm, long-term perspective, you'll see your investments grow and benefit from the magic of compounding.

# Chapter 12

# Income, Expenses, and Budgeting – The Basics of Financial Planning

Understanding how to plan finances with a particular emphasis on managing income and expenses, budgeting wisely, and creating habits that foster financial independence.

Help children create simple budgets to track their income and expenses, setting the foundation for responsible financial habits that will guide them towards wealth-building and away from destructive financial decisions.

## Introduction to Financial Planning

Financial planning is the cornerstone of personal wealth management. Whether you're a child receiving pocket money or an adult earning a salary, or self-employed, financial planning ensures that you allocate your resources efficiently, avoiding waste and maximising growth potential. At its heart, financial planning revolves around managing three primary components: **income, expenses, and savings**. Understanding these components is crucial in ensuring financial stability and avoiding pitfalls that lead to debt and financial distress.

Teaching children the basics of financial planning will help them develop healthy habits early on, building a framework they can rely on for a lifetime of financial success. The earlier they learn how to budget, save, and invest wisely, the better equipped they'll be to navigate the complexities of personal finance as adults.

# The Core of Financial Planning: Income, Expenses, and Savings

The core concept of financial planning is simple: you must ensure that your **income exceeds your expenses** to generate **savings**. These savings, when used wisely, become the building blocks for wealth accumulation through **investments**. However, if your expenses consistently exceed your income, you fall into the trap of **debt**, which leads to financial stress and wealth destruction. Understanding the balance between these components is essential.

Let's break it down into two opposing processes: **Wealth-Building** and **Wealth Destruction**.

# Wealth-Building Process

Wealth-building is a long-term journey that requires consistent discipline, responsible spending, and strategic investing. By managing your income and expenses wisely, you can create the necessary conditions for wealth growth. The formula for wealth-building is simple: **save more than you spend and invest the difference**. Let's look at the key steps in this process.

### 1. Creating a Positive Cash Flow

Active Income > Needs and Necessities

The starting point of financial success is ensuring that your **active income** exceeds your **basic needs and necessities**. Active income refers to the money you earn through work or services, such as earned money, allowances, or a salary. **Needs and necessities** include things that are essential to your well-being: food, housing, education, transportation, and healthcare.

**Formula: Active Income – Expenses (Needs and Necessities) = Savings**

**Key Insight:**

When your active income exceeds your basic expenses, you create savings. These savings are the foundation upon which wealth can grow.

## 2. Strategic Investment of Savings

Savings → Incremental Growth through Investments

Once you've saved some of your income, the next step is to **invest** that savings in productive assets. Investments could include **stocks, Index ETFs, bonds**, or even **small-scale entrepreneurial ventures**. The goal is to generate a return on your savings, allowing your money to grow over time.

**Formula: Savings + Investments (Stocks, ETFs, etc.) = Compounded Wealth**

**Key Insight:**

Saving alone isn't enough to build wealth due to inflation, which reduces the purchasing power of money over time. By investing your savings, you tap into the power of **compound interest**, where your earnings generate additional earnings.

## 3. Reinvestment for Accelerated Growth

Reinvestment is the practice of putting the returns from your investments back into the market rather than spending them. By doing so, you allow your wealth to grow exponentially. This step is crucial because reinvestment accelerates the **compounding effect**, where your earnings continue to generate more earnings over time.

**Formula: Compounded Returns + Reinvested Income = Accelerated Growth**

**Key Insight:**

The earlier and more consistently you reinvest your returns, the faster your wealth will grow. This step requires discipline, as it can be tempting to spend your returns instead of reinvesting them.

## 4. Passive Income Exceeds Active Income = Financial Freedom

The ultimate goal of wealth-building is to generate enough **passive income** from your investments to cover your living expenses. Passive income includes earnings from **dividends, interest, rental income**, or other sources that do not require you to actively work for them. When your passive income exceeds your active income, you achieve **financial freedom**. This means you can sustain your lifestyle without relying on a job or active work.

**Formula: Passive Income > Active Income = Financial Freedom**

## Key Insight

Financial freedom is the point at which your investments work for you, rather than you working for money. At this stage, you can choose to continue working or retire comfortably.

## Wealth Destruction Process

On the other hand, the process of wealth destruction happens when you fail to manage your income and expenses wisely. Poor financial habits, such as overspending on luxuries or taking on excessive debt, can erode your wealth and lead to financial instability. The wealth destruction process begins when you spend more than you earn and continues to spiral as debt accumulates and financial burdens grow.

1. **Active Income – Expenses (Including Luxuries)**

    The wealth destruction process begins when your **active income** is insufficient to cover both your **basic needs** and your **luxury expenses**. Luxuries refer to non-essential items, such as eating out, shopping, vacations, and entertainment. When you spend more than you earn, you end up borrowing money, which creates **debt**.

    **Formula: Active Income – Expenses (including Luxuries) = Debt**

    **Key Insight:**

    Luxuries should always come after saving and investing. If luxuries are prioritised over necessities, you risk accumulating debt, which is the first step towards financial trouble.

2. **Debt Accumulation → Accumulated Interest**

    Debt becomes even more dangerous when it starts to accumulate **interest**. For instance, borrowing through credit cards or loans often carries high-interest rates. If you don't pay off your debt quickly, the **interest on the debt** grows, increasing your financial burden over time. This is known as a **debt spiral**.

**Formula: Debt + Accumulated Interest = Growing Financial Burden**

**Key Insight:**

Interest on debt can grow rapidly, especially when borrowing from high-interest sources. It's crucial to pay off debts as quickly as possible to avoid falling into a debt trap.

### 3. Reduced Ability to Save or Invest

When you're constantly repaying debt and its accumulated interest, you have **less money** available to save or invest. This lack of savings prevents you from taking advantage of investment opportunities, which stunts your financial growth. Over time, this cycle can lead to **financial stagnation.**

**Formula: Debt Payments > Savings = No Investment Capital**

**Key Insight:**

If all your income is being used to repay debt, you have no capital left for investments. This halts any potential wealth-building process and keeps you stuck in a cycle of debt.

### 4. Wealth Destruction

As debt continues to grow and savings are depleted, your wealth can eventually be destroyed. In extreme cases, you may be forced to sell your assets or take on more loans to cover your financial obligations. This leads to a **destructive cycle** where it becomes increasingly difficult to recover financially.

**Formula: High Debt + Ongoing Luxuries = Wealth Destruction**

**Key Insight:**

Failing to control debt and spending can lead to financial ruin. To avoid this, it's essential to keep luxuries in check and manage debt responsibly.

# Creating a Simple Budget for Kids

To help children develop responsible financial habits, it's essential to introduce them to the concept of **budgeting** early on. A budget is a simple plan that tracks income, expenses, and savings. By teaching kids how to budget, you empower them to take control of their finances and make smart decisions.

Here's a step-by-step guide to creating a simple budget:

**Step 1: Identify Sources of Income**

The first step in creating a budget is to list all sources of **income**. For children, this might include pocket money, allowances, gifts, or income from small jobs (like babysitting or lawn mowing). Understanding where their money comes from is crucial for effective planning.

**Example:**

Monthly pocket money = ₹500

Birthday gift = ₹1,000

Small jobs (chores, babysitting, etc.) = ₹200

**Total Income** = ₹1,700

**Step 2: Track Expenses**

Next, list all **expenses**. Expenses can be broken down into two categories: **needs** (essential expenses) and **wants** (non-essential luxury items). Encourage children to prioritise their needs before spending on wants.

**Example:**

Needs:

- School supplies = ₹300
- Snacks = ₹150

Wants:

- Toys = ₹400
- Movies = ₹200

**Total Expenses** = ₹1,050

## Step 3: Calculate Savings

Once income and expenses are recorded, calculate how much money is left over for **savings**. Ideally, children should save a portion of their income each month before spending on luxuries. These savings can be used for future goals or invested in something productive.

- **Formula**:

**Income – Expenses = Savings**

- **Example:**

₹1,700 - ₹1,050 = ₹650 (available for savings)

## Step 4: Set Financial Goals

Encourage children to set specific financial goals. These goals could include saving for a new toy, a special outing, or even a long-term investment in a stock or mutual fund. Setting goals helps motivate children to stick to their budget and make thoughtful financial decisions.

- **Example:**

Goal: Save ₹2,000 for a new bicycle

Monthly Savings: ₹650

Time to Reach Goal: 3 months

## Step 5: Review and Adjust the Budget

Finally, it's important to review the budget regularly and make adjustments as necessary. Encourage children to track their spending, save consistently, and avoid overspending on non-essential items. By keeping their budget updated, they can ensure that they're on track to meet their financial goals.


# Final Thoughts: Building Strong Financial Habits

Understanding income, expenses, and budgeting is the first step towards financial independence. By teaching children how to create a simple budget, track their spending, and save for the future, you equip them with the tools they need to make smart financial decisions. Budgeting not only helps avoid debt but also lays the groundwork for wealth-building through disciplined saving and investing.

It's important to instil the idea that financial success doesn't come from how much you earn, but from how well you manage your money. When children learn to control their expenses, save for the future, and invest wisely, they set themselves on a path towards financial freedom. The lessons they learn today will have a profound impact on their financial well-being in the future.

# Chapter 13

# Learning from Mistakes – The Best Teacher in Investing

Mistakes in investing are inevitable, especially for those just beginning their journey. However, mistakes are not failures; they are opportunities to learn and refine your strategy. In this chapter, we will explore the lessons that can be drawn from errors in investing, focusing on real-life examples and case studies of successful investors who turned their missteps into long-term wins. The ability to recover from setbacks and adapt to new situations separates good investors from great ones.

**Key Focus: Case studies of successful investors who learned from their mistakes.**

Takeaway: Mistakes are part of the journey – what you learn from them matters more.

## The Power of Learning from Mistakes

Mistakes in investing are often seen as disasters, but they should be embraced as opportunities for learning and growth. Every investor, from a beginner to a seasoned professional, faces failures at some point. What defines long-term success is how you respond to those failures and evolve your strategy.

> "In investing, what is comfortable is rarely profitable."
>
> – Robert Arnott

This quote by the renowned financial researcher reminds us that taking calculated risks and making mistakes is an essential part of growing as an investor. You cannot avoid every pitfall, but you can develop the skills and mindset needed to recover, adapt, and thrive.

## Realising Mistakes is a Sign of Growth

When children or new investors first begin their journey in the financial markets, their early mistakes are often rooted in emotional decisions, a lack of research, or overconfidence. However, mistakes are also the moments when the most impactful lessons are learned.

Consider your first attempts at handling money. Maybe you spent all your pocket money in one day, leaving nothing for the rest of the week. Or maybe you missed an opportunity to save and later realised how important that habit was. Each mistake, whether small or large, is a stepping stone to financial wisdom.

## Case Study 1: Warren Buffett's Early Mistakes

Even one of the most successful investors of all time, Warren Buffett, made mistakes early in his career. One of Buffett's first investments was buying shares of a company called Cities Service Preferred. He purchased three shares at $38 per share, but the stock quickly dropped to $27. Panicked, Buffett sold his shares as soon as the price recovered slightly, making a small profit. However, the stock continued to climb to $200 per share, and Buffett realised that his hasty decision had cost him significant potential gains.

**Lesson:** Patience is key. Reacting out of fear or excitement can often lead to suboptimal decisions. It's important to maintain a long-term outlook and not get swayed by short-term fluctuations.

**Key Takeaway:** One of Buffett's biggest teachings is to "be fearful when others are greedy and greedy when others are fearful." This means making rational, rather than emotional, decisions based on thorough analysis and long-term vision.

## Emotional vs Rational Decisions

A common mistake, especially for young investors, is making emotional decisions. Markets can be volatile, and seeing your investment drop can cause panic. But reacting impulsively, whether to market ups or downs, rarely yields good results.

- *Emotional Decisions* lead to: Buying high (when prices are rising), selling low (when prices are falling), and chasing short-term trends.

- *Rational Decisions* lead to: Buying based on research, Holding through volatility, Staying committed to long-term goals.

**Actionable Item**: Next time you feel the urge to sell or buy impulsively, take a step back. Review your original reasons for investing, the long-term potential, and whether the market fluctuation is short-term noise or signals a fundamental change.

## Case Study 2: Rakesh Jhunjhunwala's Setback with Leveraged Positions

Indian billionaire investor Rakesh Jhunjhunwala is another example of someone who learned from mistakes. Jhunjhunwala, known as the "Big Bull," once incurred huge losses early in his career when he took on excessive leverage. Leveraging is borrowing money to increase potential returns, but it also magnifies risks. A small market downturn caused his leveraged positions to fail, leading to substantial losses.

**Lesson:** Leverage is a double-edged sword. While it can increase profits, it can also amplify losses. Successful investors like Jhunjhunwala learned the hard way that controlling risk is more important than chasing quick gains.

**Key Takeaway**: Jhunjhunwala's experience taught him the importance of risk management. His advice to investors is simple: "If you control your risk, your returns will take care of themselves."

## Embracing Mistakes as Part of the Process

Children and new investors should be encouraged to embrace their early mistakes. These mistakes are often the best teachers because they reveal weaknesses in our approach that we may not have noticed otherwise. They force us to reflect on our decisions, recognise patterns, and adjust strategies for the future.

**Example**: Imagine a young investor who puts all their money into a single stock because it seems like a "sure thing." When the stock price

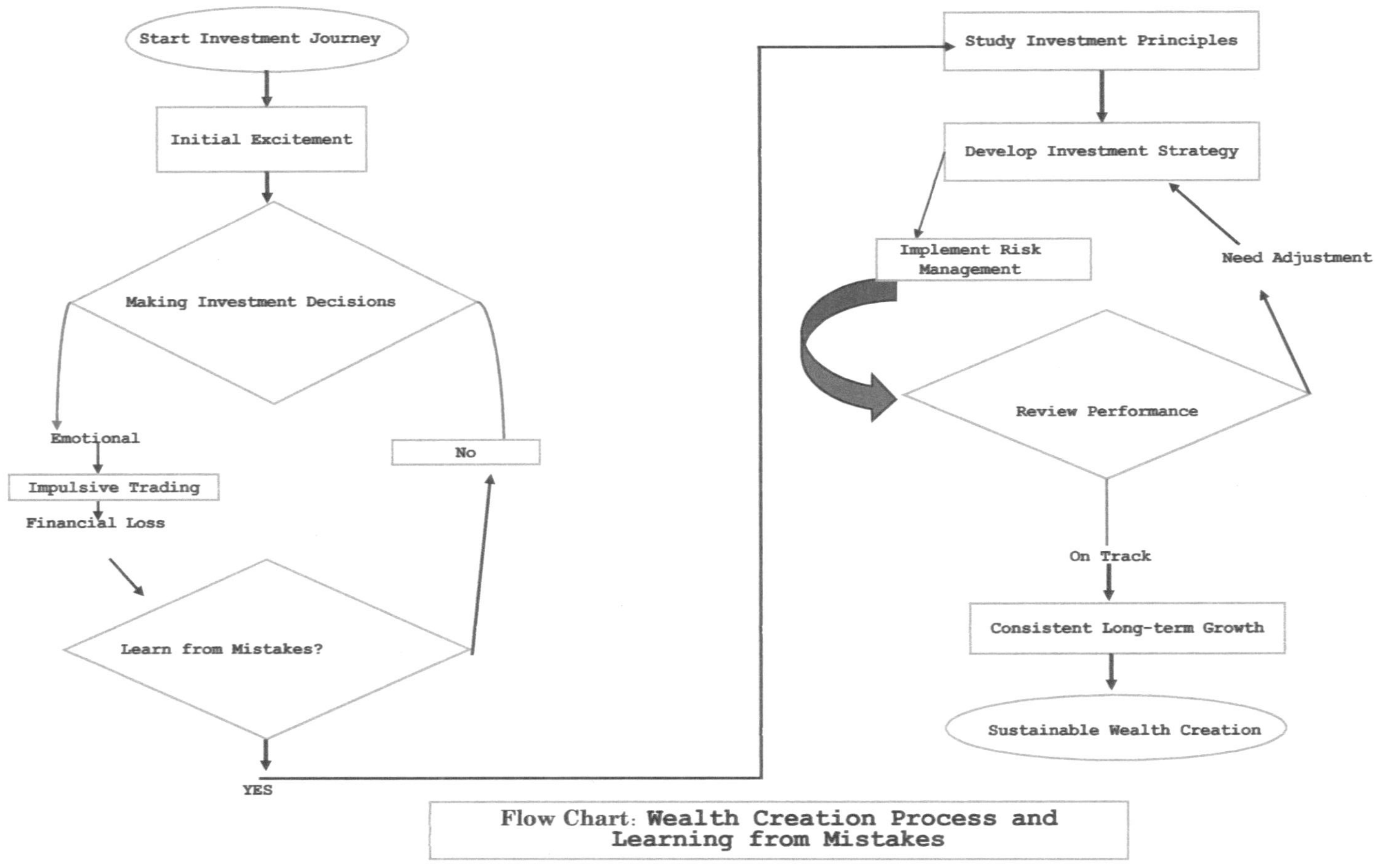
Start Investment Journey
Initial Excitement
Making Investment Decisions
Emotional
Impulsive Trading
Financial Loss
No
Learn from Mistakes?
YES
Study Investment Principles
Develop Investment Strategy
Implement Risk Management
Need Adjustment
Review Performance
On Track
Consistent Long-term Growth
Sustainable Wealth Creation
Flow Chart: Wealth Creation Process and Learning from Mistakes

falls, the investor loses a significant portion of their savings. However, this experience teaches them a valuable lesson about diversification: spreading investments across different assets reduces risk.

## Case Study 3: Peter Lynch's Rule of Research

Peter Lynch, the legendary manager of Fidelity's Magellan Fund, famously turned $20 million into $14 billion during his tenure. Despite his success, Lynch made his fair share of mistakes. In his early years, Lynch admitted to buying stocks based on "stories" or popular trends rather than doing in-depth research. This resulted in poor investment choices and some financial losses.

**Lesson:** Research is the foundation of successful investing. Don't rely on hearsay or hype – understand the companies you're investing in.

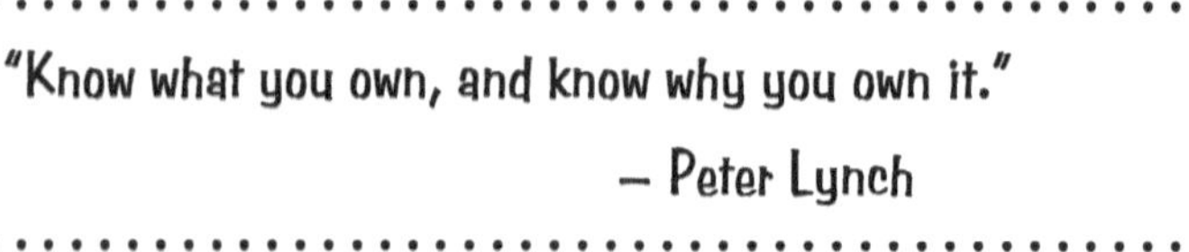


**Key Takeaway**: Peter Lynch's mistakes taught him the importance of thorough research. His approach shifted to a focus on deep analysis of company fundamentals, which allowed him to avoid poor investments and maximise long-term returns.

## Mistakes Are Opportunities for Reflection

Each mistake provides a chance to reflect on what went wrong and why. Was it poor research? Emotional decision-making? A lack of understanding about the stock market or other investment vehicles? Mistakes are often the result of a mismatch between expectations and reality, which provides a valuable opportunity to close that gap.

**Actionable Item**: After every investment decision—whether good or bad—spend time reflecting on the process. Write down why you made that decision, what factors you considered, and what you learned from the outcome.

## The Role of Experience in Overcoming Mistakes

Experience is one of the most valuable assets an investor can have. Experienced investors don't avoid mistakes, but they tend to make fewer catastrophic ones because they've learned from their previous errors. Mistakes become less frequent and less severe as they refine their strategies and adapt to market conditions.

## Case Study 4: Ray Dalio's Near Bankruptcy Experience

Ray Dalio, the founder of Bridgewater Associates, the largest hedge fund in the world, nearly went bankrupt early in his career. In the early 1980s, Dalio bet heavily that the market would crash, but his prediction was wrong. He lost so much money that he had to borrow $4,000 from his father to pay his bills.

**Lesson:** Dalio's mistake taught him the importance of humility and the value of being open to other perspectives. He developed a system of radical transparency within his company, which helped him avoid confirmation bias and improve decision-making.

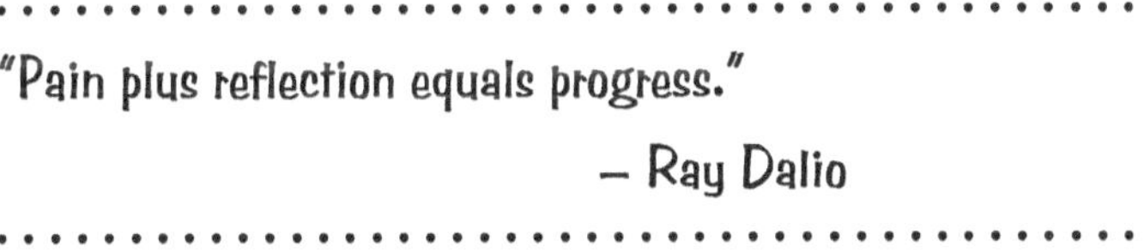


**Key Takeaway**: Dalio's mistake became a foundation for his later success. He learned to balance conviction with humility, which allowed him to recover from failure and ultimately build one of the most successful hedge funds in history.

## Turning Setbacks into Successes

The common theme in all of these stories is that mistakes are not just bumps on the road; they are essential steps toward success. Whether it's Warren Buffett learning the value of patience, Rakesh Jhunjhunwala understanding the dangers of leverage, or Ray Dalio embracing humility after a near-bankruptcy, every great investor has used their mistakes as learning experiences.

**Actionable Item**: Whenever you make a mistake, write down what you learned from it. Develop a list of "lessons learned" that you can refer back to in the future. This will help you avoid repeating the same mistakes and keep you focused on continual improvement.

## Key Takeaways

1. **Patience is Crucial**: Don't make hasty decisions based on short-term market fluctuations. Keep your focus on the long-term, and remember that most successful investors are those who can weather the ups and downs of the market.

2. **Diversify to Reduce Risk**: Putting all your eggs in one basket is a common mistake. Spreading your investments across various assets helps protect against large losses.

3. **Emotional Control**: The stock market can be volatile, but making decisions out of fear or excitement will usually lead to poor outcomes. Practice emotional discipline and make decisions based on research.

4. **Learn from Every Mistake**: Every mistake is an opportunity for growth. Reflect on what went wrong and apply those lessons to your future investments.

5. **Don't Follow Hype**: Invest in what you understand. Just because a stock or investment is popular doesn't mean it's right for you. Always do your research.

6. **Embrace Humility**: Even the most experienced investors make mistakes. The key is to remain humble, stay open to new perspectives, and be willing to adapt.

## Conclusion: Turning Failure into Future Success

In investing, mistakes are inevitable, but they are also some of the best teachers you will encounter. By learning from your errors and understanding the lessons hidden in each setback, you will be better prepared to make smarter, more informed decisions in the future.

Investing is a long journey, and every mistake, large or small, provides a valuable lesson that brings you closer to long-term success.

# Chapter 14

# Setting Long-Term Goals: The Path to Financial Independence

Setting long-term goals is a critical aspect of financial planning and personal development. It provides a roadmap for future achievements, whether it's for education, travel, or significant life events. For young learners, understanding how to create and follow through with long-term goals can significantly impact their financial independence and personal success. In this chapter, we'll explore how to help kids set achievable goals, teach them the power of planning, and give them the tools they need to stay motivated on their path toward financial independence.

## Why Setting Long-Term Goals Matters

Long-term goals give direction to our actions. Without a clear target in mind, it becomes easy to drift through life, making decisions that don't serve a larger purpose. For children and teenagers, setting long-term goals helps them focus on future success, whether it's saving for college, starting a business, or planning for a dream trip. Goals provide motivation and a sense of purpose, allowing young people to make smarter financial choices early on.

Financial independence doesn't happen overnight. It requires a series of well-thought-out decisions and actions over time. That's where long-term goals come into play. By establishing clear goals, young learners can visualise their journey toward financial freedom and break down this seemingly overwhelming task into manageable steps.

## The SMART Framework for Goal-Setting

One of the most effective ways to teach children how to set long-term goals is by using the SMART framework. SMART stands for:

- Specific: Goals should be clear and well-defined.
- Measurable: Progress can be tracked with concrete indicators.
- Attainable: The goal must be realistic and achievable.
- Relevant: The goal should matter to the individual's larger plans.
- Time-bound: Goals need a deadline to provide motivation.

**Example**: If a teen wants to save ₹50,000 for a trip, instead of saying, "I want to save money," they could set a SMART goal like, "I will save ₹50,000 in two years by setting aside ₹2,100 per month from my part-time job."

## Case Study: How Ratan Tata Built Long-Term Goals

Ratan Tata, one of India's most respected business leaders, is an excellent example of how long-term goals, combined with dedication, can lead to success. When Tata took over the Tata Group, the company was seen as conservative and slow-growing. However, he had long-term goals for transforming the group into a global player. With a series of calculated decisions—such as the acquisition of Jaguar Land Rover and Tetley Tea—Tata expanded the company's reach across the world.

What made Tata's strategy remarkable was his focus on long-term sustainability and social responsibility. He didn't chase quick profits but invested in initiatives that would bear fruit over decades. This is the mindset young learners should develop: the ability to think beyond short-term rewards and focus on sustained growth.

## The Importance of Financial Goals in Achieving Independence

Financial independence refers to the point at which someone's passive income (from investments, savings, or businesses) exceeds their living expenses. To reach this level of freedom, long-term financial goals are essential.

**Types of Financial Goals**

- **Short-term goals**: Saving for a bicycle, a laptop, or a summer camp.
- **Medium-term goals**: Saving for college, a car, or a dream trip.

- **Long-term goals**: Building a portfolio for financial independence, saving for retirement, or buying a house.

**Actionable Item**: Help children categorise their goals into short, medium, and long-term. For each goal, estimate the amount of money needed and the timeframe. This allows them to better understand what they're working towards and how to allocate their resources.

## Breaking Down Long-Term Goals into Manageable Steps

One of the most common mistakes in goal-setting is making goals too broad or unrealistic. The key is to break down big goals into smaller, manageable steps. These steps provide a clear path forward and make the journey feel more achievable.

**Example**: Let's say a teen's long-term goal is to save ₹200,000 for college over four years. This can be broken down into smaller goals, such as:

- Save ₹50,000 per year.

- Set aside ₹4,200 per month.

- Find a part-time job or freelance work to help meet this target.

By breaking down large goals into smaller actions, children and teenagers can focus on daily or monthly tasks without feeling overwhelmed.

## Motivation and Perseverance: Sticking to the Plan

One of the most significant challenges young learners will face is staying motivated over time. Long-term goals, by definition, take years to achieve, and it's easy to lose focus along the way.

## Key Strategies for Staying Motivated

- **Celebrate Small Wins**: Every time a milestone is reached, take time to celebrate. Whether it's hitting a savings target or making a wise investment, acknowledging these achievements keeps morale high.

- **Track Progress**: Use tools like a budget tracker, journal, or app to monitor progress. This not only helps in staying organised but also provides motivation when they see how far they've come.

- **Stay Flexible**: Life is unpredictable, and sometimes goals need to be adjusted. It's important to stay flexible and adapt plans as needed. If one approach isn't working, try another, but never lose sight of the long-term vision.

## Case Study: Warren Buffett's Long-Term Investment Strategy

A prime example of the magic of long-term investment is Warren Buffett. By investing from a very young age and allowing his returns to reinvest and grow over time, Buffett's wealth has exploded in his later years. In fact, **99% of Warren Buffett's wealth was earned after the age of 50**, showing the power of compounding over time.

The key takeaway for young investors and parents teaching kids about wealth-building is simple: start early, stay consistent, and **let your investments grow for as long as possible**. Whether through continuous or regular compounding, the results will speak for themselves.

Buffett's approach wasn't to get rich quick but to grow his wealth steadily over decades by investing in companies with solid fundamentals. He avoided trends and fads, opting instead for companies with proven track records and sustainable business models. His long-term mindset is an ideal lesson for young learners aiming for financial independence. They should prioritise patience and consistency over chasing immediate gratification.

## Diagram: The Path to Financial Independence Through Goal-Setting

- **Step 1**: Set a SMART goal (e.g., Save ₹1,00,000 in 3 years for a laptop)

- **Step 2**: Break it down (e.g. Save ₹2,800 per month)

- **Step 3**: Take action (e.g., get a part-time job or set aside birthday money)

- **Step 4**: Track progress (e.g. Use a savings tracker)

- **Step 5**: Adjust as necessary (e.g. if expenses go up, adjust the monthly target)

- **Step 6**: Celebrate when the goal is reached (e.g., Buy the laptop!)

This simple yet effective process helps young learners visualise the path towards achieving their financial goals, making the journey seem less daunting.

## Common Mistakes When Setting Long-Term Goals

Even with the best intentions, mistakes happen. Some common mistakes include:

- **Being too vague**: A goal like "I want to be rich" is too ambiguous. Instead, frame it in specific terms (e.g., "I want to save ₹1,00,000 by the time I'm 18").

- **Not having a plan**: Without a step-by-step plan, long-term goals are harder to achieve. Break the goal into smaller, more manageable tasks.

- **Lack of flexibility**: Life happens. If circumstances change, adjust your goals but don't abandon them.

**Actionable Item**: Encourage kids to regularly review their goals. If something changes (e.g. a new interest or unexpected expense), they can adjust their goals without feeling like they've failed.

## The Role of Parents and Mentors in Goal-Setting

Parents, teachers, and mentors play a crucial role in guiding children through the process of setting long-term goals. It's important for adults to support the child's vision and encourage them along the way, but not to set the goals for them.

## Actionable Items for Parents

- **Ask questions**: Encourage children to think about what they want and why. Ask them what they hope to achieve in the future and how they plan to get there.

- **Provide resources**: Whether it's helping them set up a savings account or introducing them to investment tools, make sure they have the resources they need to reach their goals.

- **Celebrate achievements**: When your child reaches a milestone, celebrate it. This will reinforce the value of hard work and perseverance.

. . . . . . . . . . . . . . . . . . . . . . . . . . . . . . . . . . . . . . . . .

*"If you fail to plan, you are planning to fail."*

— Benjamin Franklin

. . . . . . . . . . . . . . . . . . . . . . . . . . . . . . . . . . . . . . . . .

- This famous quote by Benjamin Franklin highlights the importance of planning in achieving long-term goals. For young learners, understanding that success doesn't happen by accident but through deliberate planning and effort can be a transformative lesson.

## Key Takeaways

- **Long-term goals** provide direction and motivation.

- Use the **SMART framework** to make goals specific, measurable, attainable, relevant, and time-bound.

- Break down large goals into **smaller, manageable steps**.

- Stay motivated by celebrating small wins and **tracking progress**.

- **Learn from mistakes** and adjust your goals when necessary.

- Parents and mentors should provide **support and encouragement**, but allow children to set their own goals.

By teaching kids and teenagers how to set long-term goals, we equip them with the tools they need to take control of their financial future. These lessons will not only help them achieve their immediate goals but also set them on a path towards lifelong financial independence.

# Chapter 15

# Growing the Wealth Infinity Cycle: Beyond Investments

The journey towards financial independence doesn't end once you've started saving and investing. In fact, the real magic begins when you understand how to grow your wealth beyond just investments – how to build passive income streams, how to make your money work for you continuously, and how to achieve financial freedom that lasts a lifetime. This chapter explores advanced strategies that take you beyond the basics of investing and into the realms of wealth expansion, compounding, and financial legacy building. We'll also dive into the concept of *"The Wealth Infinity Cycle,"* which underscores how to keep your financial growth sustained indefinitely.

## What is the Wealth Infinity Cycle?

The Wealth Infinity Cycle represents a continuous loop of disciplined saving, investing, reinvesting, and growth. The idea is to create a self-sustaining system where your investments generate enough returns to fuel further investments. This cycle, once initiated, becomes self-perpetuating and leads to long-term financial freedom.

## The Components of the Wealth Infinity Cycle

1. **Save Regularly**: Develop a habit of saving a fixed percentage of your income.

2. **Invest Consistently**: Use your savings to invest in assets that grow in value over time.

3. **Reinvest Returns**: Instead of spending the gains, reinvest them to create compounding growth.

4. **Increase Capital**: As your wealth grows, increase the amount you save and invest.

5. **Enjoy Financial Independence**: Over time, your wealth generates enough income to sustain your lifestyle without active labour.

This is the power of long-term financial planning: your wealth becomes a renewable resource.

## Why Go Beyond Basic Investments?

While basic investing (such as stocks, bonds, or ETFs) is a fantastic starting point for building wealth, there are additional ways to accelerate financial growth. Going beyond simple investments means diversifying into alternative assets, creating passive income streams, and understanding how to leverage your money for bigger returns.

## Key Benefits of Expanding Your Investment Strategy

- **Diversification**: Helps reduce risk by not relying on just one type of investment.

- **Higher Returns**: Certain advanced investments can yield higher returns than traditional stock market investments.

- **Passive Income**: You can create streams of income that don't require active work (e.g., real estate, dividends).

- **Financial Security**: A well-rounded portfolio provides protection against market volatility and economic downturns.

## Types of Investments Beyond Stocks and Bonds

While stocks, bonds, and ETFs provide a solid foundation, growing your wealth in a sustainable manner requires branching out into other forms of investments.

## 1. Real Estate

Investing in real estate is one of the most popular ways to grow wealth. Real estate can provide both rental income (passive income) and long-term capital appreciation. It also acts as a hedge against inflation since property values tend to rise over time.

**Example**: Imagine purchasing a property for ₹50,00,000. After renting it out, you receive ₹20,000 per month in rental income, while the property itself appreciates to ₹65,00,000 over five years. You've not only gained rental income but also experienced capital growth.

## 2. Dividend-Paying Stocks

Stocks that pay regular dividends offer another form of passive income. Unlike growth stocks, which reinvest profits into the company, dividend-paying stocks distribute a portion of profits directly to shareholders.

**Actionable Item**: Teach children how to look for companies that have a strong track record of paying dividends. By reinvesting these dividends back into the market, they can take advantage of compounding returns.

## 3. Index Funds & ETFs

While already mentioned in earlier chapters, it's worth revisiting index funds and ETFs from a long-term perspective. These financial vehicles allow you to invest in a diversified set of companies, reducing risk and promoting steady growth over time.

**Case Study**: Warren Buffett has famously advocated for index funds as a smart, low-cost way to invest. In 2008, he made a $1 million bet that a basic S&P 500 index fund would outperform a group of hedge funds over ten years. In 2017, Buffett won the bet. The index fund had averaged a 7.1% annual gain, while the hedge funds averaged only 2.2%.

## 4. Mutual Funds with a Growth Focus

Growth-oriented mutual funds pool money from multiple investors to purchase shares in companies expected to grow at an above-average rate compared to other companies. This is a good option for those who want a diversified portfolio managed by professionals but are willing to take on more risk for higher returns.

### 5. Peer-to-Peer Lending

Peer-to-peer lending allows you to lend money directly to individuals or small businesses through online platforms. In return, you receive interest on the loan. This is riskier than traditional savings or investing, but it can offer higher returns.

### 6. Business Ventures

If you're entrepreneurial, investing in or starting a business can be one of the most lucrative paths to financial independence. Businesses, especially scalable ones, can generate significant income streams.

**Actionable Item**: Encourage kids to start small ventures like online businesses, side hustles, or freelancing. This helps them develop an entrepreneurial mindset, which is crucial for wealth growth.

## Reinvesting: The Key to Accelerating Growth

Reinvestment is the process of taking the returns you've earned from one investment and putting them back into another—or the same—investment to generate even more returns. This creates a compounding effect, accelerating your financial growth.

## How Compounding Works in the Wealth Infinity Cycle

1. **Initial Investment**: You invest ₹10,000 in a stock or mutual fund.

2. **Earnings**: Over the next year, you earn ₹1,000 in returns.

3. **Reinvest**: Instead of spending that ₹1,000, you reinvest it.

4. **Growth**: The next year, you now have ₹11,000 working for you, which earns even more returns.

This cycle of reinvesting returns continues to build, creating exponential growth over time.

## Diagram: The Wealth Infinity Cycle

Step 1: Save → Step 2: Invest → Step 3: Reinvest Earnings → Step 4: Grow → Step 5: Increase Capital

The key to the Wealth Infinity Cycle is that it never stops. You're always saving, investing, and reinvesting, which keeps your money working for you indefinitely.

## Avoiding Wealth Destruction: The Opposite of the Wealth Infinity Cycle

While the Wealth Infinity Cycle focuses on growth, there is also a reverse cycle that leads to wealth destruction. This occurs when people fail to reinvest or make poor financial decisions that erode their wealth over time.

## How Wealth Destruction Happens

1. **Overspending**: Instead of saving and investing, spending money on depreciating assets such as luxury items, cars, or expensive gadgets.

2. **Debt Accumulation**: Taking on high-interest debt such as credit cards or personal loans and being unable to pay them off.

3. **Lack of Investment**: Keeping money in low-interest savings accounts instead of investing it, leading to lost opportunities for growth.

4. **Ignoring Inflation**: If your money isn't growing at a rate faster than inflation, it's actually losing value.

**Actionable Item**: Teach children about the dangers of overspending and debt. Show them how to track their expenses and stay disciplined with their financial goals.

## Case Study: The Fall of Lehman Brothers

The collapse of Lehman Brothers in 2008 is a prime example of how poor financial decisions can lead to wealth destruction. Once one of the largest investment banks in the world, Lehman took on excessive risk through bad loans and investments in the housing market. When the housing bubble burst, Lehman couldn't cover its liabilities, leading to the largest bankruptcy filing in U.S. history.

The lesson here is that reckless investing without proper risk management can lead to catastrophic losses – even for the biggest players in the market. This applies to individuals as well; if we don't respect financial discipline, we risk losing everything.

## Growing Beyond Financial Independence: Passive Income and Legacy Building

Once financial independence is achieved, the next step is to grow your wealth even further by creating passive income streams and thinking about long-term legacy planning.

## Ways to Grow Beyond Financial Independence

- **Real Estate Rental Income**: Owning multiple properties can generate a continuous stream of passive income.

- **Dividend Payments**: High-dividend stocks can replace a salary once you've built a significant portfolio.

- **Online Businesses**: Creating digital products or subscription-based services can generate passive income with minimal effort after the initial setup.

- **Building a Legacy**: Consider estate planning, trusts, and charitable donations to leave a financial legacy for future generations.

**Actionable Item**: Introduce young learners to the concept of creating a will or trust early in life. It helps them understand that wealth isn't just about living comfortably, but also about ensuring the well-being of future generations.

> "Do not save what is left after spending;
> instead spend what is left after saving."
>
> – Warren Buffett

This quote from Warren Buffett reinforces the importance of prioritising saving and investing over spending. It's a key principle in the Wealth Infinity Cycle: the more disciplined you are about saving, the faster your wealth will grow.

## Key Takeaways

- The Wealth Infinity Cycle is a self-sustaining system where savings, investment, and reinvestment lead to exponential growth.

Expanding beyond basic investments is crucial to accelerating financial growth. Consider options like real estate, dividend-paying stocks, and business ventures.

- Reinvesting returns creates the power of compounding, allowing wealth to grow faster over time.

- Avoid wealth destruction by maintaining financial discipline, avoiding high debt, and always planning for inflation.

- Once you achieve financial independence, focus on growing passive income streams and building a lasting financial legacy.

With this chapter, you've gained insight into how the Wealth Infinity Cycle can be the foundation for a lifetime of financial success. It's not just about getting rich quickly; it's about consistent, disciplined growth that ensures you and future generations thrive financially.

# Chapter 16

# Exploring Portfolio Management Services (PMS)

As your financial journey matures, you will encounter investment tools and strategies that go beyond traditional avenues like mutual funds, index ETFs, or even individual stocks. One such advanced financial tool is **Portfolio Management Services (PMS)**, designed for investors seeking tailored strategies, professional expertise, and robust wealth management.

In this chapter, we will explore PMS in depth, understanding its nuances, benefits, limitations, and how it aligns with the vision of achieving *Wealth Infinity*.

## What is Portfolio Management Services (PMS)?

Portfolio Management Services, often referred to as PMS, is a professional investment service where a dedicated portfolio manager or firm manages your investments on your behalf. Unlike mutual funds, which pool money from many investors into a single portfolio, PMS provides a customized investment strategy, tailored to your individual financial goals, risk appetite, and time horizon.

PMS is often seen as the next step for high-net-worth individuals (HNIs) who wish to have a more personalized approach to wealth management. It bridges the gap between traditional investment products and bespoke financial advisory services.

## Types of Portfolio Management Services

PMS is broadly categorized into three types, each catering to different investor preferences:

1. **Discretionary PMS**
   - In a discretionary PMS, the portfolio manager has full autonomy to make investment decisions on behalf of the client.

- The manager selects, buys, and sells securities without requiring prior approval for each transaction.

- This is ideal for investors who trust the expertise of the portfolio manager and prefer a hands-off approach.

## 2. Non-Discretionary PMS

- In a non-discretionary PMS, the portfolio manager provides recommendations, but the client retains full control over investment decisions.

- The manager acts as an advisor, and no transaction is executed without the client's consent.

- This suits investors who want professional guidance but prefer to remain actively involved in decision-making.

## 3. Advisory PMS

- The portfolio manager provides comprehensive advice on asset allocation and portfolio construction, but the client executes the investments independently.

- This model is suitable for investors with a strong understanding of markets who seek strategic advice without handing over control.

# Key Features of PMS

1. **Customization:** Unlike one-size-fits-all mutual funds, PMS offers tailor-made investment strategies that align with your unique financial goals, risk tolerance, and time horizon.

2. **Professional Management:** Managed by seasoned professionals, PMS leverages deep market insights and expertise to maximize returns while mitigating risks.

3. **Diversification:** PMS portfolios often include a mix of equities, fixed income, real estate, and alternative investments, ensuring a well-balanced portfolio.

4. **Transparency:** Regular updates, reports, and performance analyses ensure you remain informed about your investments.

5. **Active Monitoring:** Continuous monitoring and rebalancing of the portfolio to adapt to changing market conditions.

## Who Should Consider PMS?

PMS is not for everyone. It is a premium investment service designed for investors with specific needs and a substantial investable corpus. Here's who it benefits the most:

1. **High-Net-Worth Individuals (HNIs):**

   PMS typically requires a minimum investment of ₹50 lakhs or more, making it ideal for HNIs looking for personalized investment strategies.

2. **Busy Professionals:**

   Individuals who lack the time or expertise to manage their investments but want professional oversight.

3. **Seasoned Investors:**

   Those who have outgrown traditional investment products and are seeking advanced strategies to optimize their portfolios.

4. **Long-Term Wealth Builders:**

   Investors with long-term financial goals, such as retirement planning, wealth preservation, or legacy creation.

## Advantages of PMS

1. **Personalized Investment Strategies:**

   PMS portfolios are crafted specifically for you, taking into account your financial objectives, risk appetite, and time frame.

2. **Expertise and Active Management:**

   Professional portfolio managers continuously monitor and adjust your investments to optimize returns and minimize risks.

### 3. Flexibility in Asset Selection:

Unlike mutual funds, PMS is not constrained by strict guidelines, allowing managers to explore diverse asset classes, including niche opportunities.

### 4. Tax Efficiency:

PMS strategies can be structured to optimize tax liabilities, such as harvesting capital losses to offset gains.

### 5. Transparency and Control:

Detailed reports and regular updates provide clarity about your portfolio's performance, holdings, and changes.

### 6. Wealth Preservation:

With a focus on risk management and diversification, PMS aims to preserve and grow wealth over time.

## Challenges and Drawbacks of PMS

### 1. High Entry Barriers:

The minimum investment threshold, usually ₹50 lakhs or higher, excludes many retail investors.

### 2. Cost:

PMS charges include management fees, performance fees, and sometimes brokerage charges, which can be significantly higher than mutual funds.

### 3. Market Risks:

Like all market-linked investments, PMS is subject to volatility and potential capital loss.

### 4. Dependence on Manager Expertise:

The success of a PMS heavily depends on the skill and experience of the portfolio manager. Poor decisions can lead to suboptimal performance.

## 5. **Illiquidity:**

While PMS offers flexibility, some strategies may involve investments in less liquid assets, which could affect your ability to access funds quickly.

# How to Choose the Right PMS Provider

Selecting the right PMS provider is critical to achieving your financial goals. Consider the following factors:

1. **Track Record:**

   - Review the historical performance of the PMS across different market cycles.

   - Look for consistency and the ability to generate alpha (excess returns).

2. **Investment Philosophy:**

   - Understand the provider's investment approach, whether it's growth-oriented, value-driven, or focused on sectoral themes.

   - Ensure it aligns with your financial objectives.

3. **Transparency:**

   - Opt for a provider that offers clear reporting on portfolio performance, fees, and holdings.

4. **Fee Structure:**

   - Understand the cost components, including management fees, performance-linked fees, and hidden charges.

   - Compare providers to ensure value for money.

5. **Reputation and Expertise:**

   - Research the provider's credentials, experience, and client testimonials.

   - Choose firms with a strong reputation in the financial industry.

# Regulatory Framework for PMS in India

In India, PMS is regulated by the **Securities and Exchange Board of India (SEBI)**. SEBI ensures transparency, accountability, and investor protection. Key regulations include:

- Minimum investment threshold of ₹50 lakhs.

- Regular performance disclosures and reporting.

- Restrictions on leveraging and short-selling.

- Mandated segregation of client funds and securities.

These regulations aim to maintain high standards of integrity and professionalism in the PMS industry.

# When to Consider PMS in Your Wealth Journey

For most investors, PMS is not the first step but a progression as their wealth grows and investment needs become more complex. Here are signs that you might be ready for PMS:

1. Your investment portfolio exceeds ₹50 lakhs.

2. You seek professional expertise to manage diverse and complex investments.

3. You want to shift from passive to active wealth management.

4. You are aiming for specific financial goals, such as legacy planning or global diversification.

# Case Study: PMS in Action

Let's illustrate the potential of PMS through a hypothetical example:

**Investor Profile:**

- Name: Arjun Sharma

- Age: 45

- Profession: Business Owner

- Investable Surplus: ₹1.5 crore

- Goals: Retirement planning, wealth preservation, and tax efficiency.

**PMS Strategy:**

- **Asset Allocation:** 60% in equities (focused on blue-chip and growth stocks), 30% in fixed income, and 10% in alternative assets like REITs.

- **Risk Management:** Diversification across sectors and geographies to reduce volatility.

- **Tax Optimization:** Structured investments to minimize tax outflows on capital gains.

**Outcome:**

Over a 10-year horizon, Arjun's portfolio achieves an annualized return of 12%, helping him comfortably meet his retirement goals while preserving capital.

## Conclusion

Portfolio Management Services (PMS) is a powerful tool for investors ready to take their wealth-building journey to the next level. By providing customized strategies, professional management, and active monitoring, PMS empowers you to achieve your financial aspirations while navigating the complexities of the investment world.

However, like any financial decision, choosing PMS requires careful evaluation of your needs, readiness, and the provider's credentials. When used effectively, PMS can be a cornerstone in your quest for *Wealth Infinity*, helping you grow, preserve, and pass on your wealth for generations to come.

## Closing Notes to the Book

Congratulations on reaching the end of *"Journey to Wealth Infinity!"* This book represents more than a collection of financial strategies—it is a blueprint for your personal transformation, guiding you from the basics of saving to mastering the art of wealth creation and preservation.

By reading this book, you've equipped yourself with the knowledge and tools necessary to take control of your financial destiny. Remember, wealth building is not a sprint but a marathon. It's a lifelong journey of learning, adapting, and staying disciplined.

The key takeaways from this book are clear:

1. Develop a strong financial foundation through disciplined saving and intelligent money habits.

2. Leverage the power of compounding and start early.

3. Master market fundamentals and invest with clarity, patience, and purpose.

4. Plan for the long term while adapting to market trends and personal goals.

5. Transition to advanced strategies like Portfolio Management Services when your financial journey demands sophisticated solutions.

Ultimately, financial independence is not about chasing wealth for its own sake. It's about creating the freedom to live life on your terms, to pursue your passions, and to secure the future for yourself and your loved ones.

This book is about more than just financial strategies—it's about building a mindset that empowers you to take control of your finances, invest wisely, and grow your wealth sustainably.

Through each chapter, we've explored the key pillars of financial success:

- Developing strong financial habits and understanding the basics of money management.

- Learning how to start investing and growing your wealth through disciplined strategies.

- Gaining the wisdom to navigate market uncertainties and align your investments with long-term goals.

The ultimate takeaway is that achieving financial freedom isn't about shortcuts or quick wins. It's about making informed decisions, staying consistent, and continually improving your financial knowledge and skills.

Your journey doesn't end here—it evolves. Whether you're just starting to save or exploring advanced strategies like Portfolio Management Services (PMS), the principles in this book will serve as your guide.

## A Personal Note from the Author

This book is a culmination of years of learning, teaching, and real-life experience. My hope is that it becomes a trusted companion in your financial journey, offering clarity when markets are confusing, inspiration when discipline feels challenging, and guidance when the road ahead is uncertain.

As you continue on this path, remember that the goal of wealth is not just accumulation but the ability to lead a fulfilling and meaningful life.

Your journey to *Wealth Infinity* is unique, and the steps you take today will shape the financial freedom you enjoy tomorrow. Trust in the process, remain consistent, and always keep learning.

**Thank you for allowing me to be part of your journey.**
**Wishing you success, abundance, and a life of purpose!**